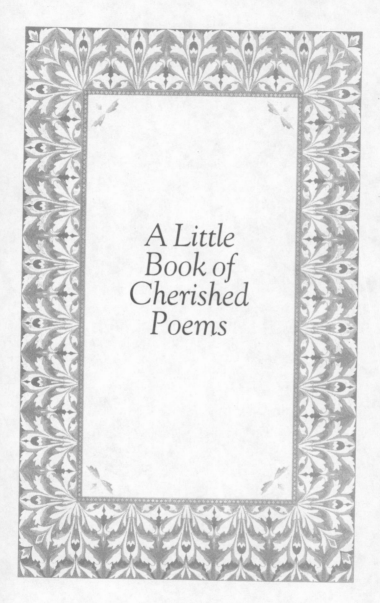

A Little
Book of
Cherished
Poems

A Little Book of Cherished Poems

BEAUTIFUL POETRY
TO TREASURE

Compiled by
KAY ANNE CARSON

GALAHAD BOOKS
NEW YORK

For Jim and Andrea—
Cherish each other.

First Galahad Books edition published in 2000.

Galahad Books
A division of BBS Publishing Corporation
386 Park Avenue South
New York, NY 10016

Galahad Books is a registered trademark of BBS Publishing Corporation.

Library of Congress Catalog Card Number: 99-97131

ISBN: 1-57866-060-2

Printed in the United States of America.

Acknowledgments

"Appraisal" reprinted with the permission of Simon and Schuster from *The Collected Poems of Sara Teasdale*. Copyright © 1926 by Macmillan Publishing Company, renewed 1954 by Mamie T. Wheless.

"Dirge without Music" by Edna St. Vincent Millay. From *Collected Poems*, HarperCollins Publishers. Copyright © 1928, 1955 by Edna St. Vincent Millay and Norma Millay Ellis. Reprinted by permission of Elizabeth Barnett, literary executor.

"Leisure", "Money" Copyright © 1963 by Jonathan Cape, Ltd. Reprinted from *The Complete Works of W.H. Davies*. Courtesy of the Estate of W.H. Davies and Jonathan Cape, Ltd.

"Nothing Gold Can Stay" from *The Poetry of Robert Frost* edited by Edward Connery Lathem. Copyright 1951 by Robert Frost. Copyright 1923 © 1969 by Henry Holt and Co., Inc. Reprinted by permission of Henry Holt and Co., Inc.

"On Friendship", "On Love", "On Marriage", reprinted from *The Prophet*, by Kahlil Gibran, by permission of Alfred A. Knopf, Inc. Copyright © 1923 by Kahlil Gibran and renewed in 1951 by Administrators C.T.A. of Kahlil Gibran Estate, and by Mary Gibran.

"To Youth" reprinted from *In American: The Collected Poems of John V.A. Weaver*, by John V.A. Weaver, by permission of Alfred A. Knopf, Inc. Copyright © 1928 and renewed 1965 by Margaret Wood Walling.

Contents

Foreword

With a rhythm that mirrors a heartbeat, poems have the power to capture the essence of all we have experienced and preserve it long past the moment. Each of the poems in this treasury was chosen for the strength of the memories they hold and their ability to wake similar memories within each of us. Whether it is the joy of a child's conquest, the innocence of young love, or the undying hope of the faithful, you will find much to reflect on between the covers of this book.

As you open these pages and walk the path they lead you, relive Robert Louis Stevenson's imaginative discovery of "Foreign Lands" through the eyes of a child viewing the world from the treetops. Reflect with William Wordsworth on an angelic beauty in "She Was a Phantom of Delight." Ponder the possibilities with Henry Wadsworth Longfellow on "My Lost Youth."

With the varied lyrical cadences of Shakespeare, Browning, Keats, Kipling, Thoreau, and other favorite poets, you will find many voices sounding varied moods. May you look within yourself and find your own memories revived by the pulse of these eternal treasures.

MSL

Youth

Nothing Gold Can Stay

Nature's first green is gold,
Her hardest hue to hold.
Her early leaf's a flower;
But only so an hour.
Then leaf subsides to leaf.
So Eden sank to grief,
So dawn goes down to day.
Nothing gold can stay.

ROBERT FROST

Sweet and low, sweet and low,
 Wind of the western sea,
Low, low, breathe and blow,
 Wind of the western sea!
Over the rolling waters go,
Come from the dying moon, and blow,
 Blow him again to me;
While my little one, while my pretty one, sleeps.

Sleep and rest, sleep and rest,
 Father will come to thee soon;
Rest, rest, on mother's breast,
 Father will come to thee soon;
Father will come to his babe in the nest,
Silver sails all out of the west
 Under the silver moon:
Sleep, my little one, sleep, my pretty one, sleep.

ALFRED, LORD TENNYSON

Between the dark and the daylight,
 When the night is beginning to lower,
Comes a pause in the day's occupations,
 That is known as the Children's Hour.

I hear in the chamber above me
 The patter of little feet,
The sound of a door that is opened,
 And voices soft and sweet.

From my study I see in the lamplight,
 Descending the broad hall stair,
Grave Alice, and laughing Allegra,
 And Edith with golden hair.

A whisper, and then a silence:
 Yet I know by their merry eyes
They are plotting and planning together
 To take me by surprise.

A sudden rush from the stairway,
 A sudden raid from the hall!
By three doors left unguarded
 They enter my castle wall!

They climb up into my turret
 O'er the arms and back of my chair;
If I try to escape, they surround me;
 They seem to be everywhere.

They almost devour me with kisses,
  Their arms about me entwine,
Till I think of the Bishop of Bingen
  In his Mouse-Tower on the Rhine!

Do you think, O blue-eyed banditti,
  Because you have scaled the wall,
Such an old mustache as I am
  Is not a match for you all!

I have you fast in my fortress,
  And will not let you depart,
But put you down into the dungeon
  In the round-tower of my heart.

And there will I keep you forever,
  Yes, forever and a day,
Till the walls shall crumble to ruin,
  And moulder in dust away!

HENRY WADSWORTH LONGFELLOW

"I Am Lonely"

From "The Spanish Gypsy"

The world is great: the birds all fly from me,
The stars are golden fruit upon a tree
All out of reach: my little sister went,
    And I am lonely.

The world is great: I tried to mount the hill
Above the pines, where the light lies so still,
But it rose higher: little Lisa went
    And I am lonely.

The world is great: the wind comes rushing by.
I wonder where it comes from; sea birds cry
And hurt my heart: my little sister went,
    And I am lonely.

The world is great: the people laugh and talk,
And make loud holiday: how fast they walk!
I'm lame, they push me: little Lisa went,
    And I am lonely.

GEORGE ELIOT

My Bed Is a Boat

My bed is like a little boat;
    Nurse helps me in when I embark;
She girds me in my sailor's coat
    And starts me in the dark.

At night, I go on board and say
    Good night to all my friends on shore;
I shut my eyes and sail away
    And see and hear no more.

And sometimes things to bed I take,
    As prudent sailors have to do;
Perhaps a slice of wedding-cake,
    Perhaps a toy or two.

All night across the dark we steer;
    But when the day returns at last,
Safe in my room, beside the pier,
    I find my vessel fast.

ROBERT LOUIS STEVENSON

"What Does Little Birdie Say?"

From "Sea Dreams"

What does little birdie say
In her nest at peep of day?
Let me fly, says little birdie,
Mother, let me fly away.
Birdie, rest a little longer,
Till the little wings are stronger.
So she rests a little longer,
Then she flies away.

What does little baby say,
In her bed at peep of day?
Baby says, like little birdie,
Let me rise and fly away.
Baby, sleep a little longer,
Till the little limbs are stronger,
If she sleeps a little longer,
Baby too shall fly away.

ALFRED, LORD TENNYSON

Nurse's Song

When the voices of children are heard on the green
   And laughing is heard on the hill,
My heart is at rest within my breast,
   And everything else is still.

"Then come home, my children, the sun is gone down,
   And the dews of the night arise;
Come, come, leave off play, and let us away
   Till the morning appears in the skies."

"No, no, let us play, for it is yet day,
   And we cannot go to sleep;
Besides in the sky the little birds fly,
   And the hills are all covered with sheep."

"Well, well, go and play till the light fades away,
   And then go home to bed."
The little ones leaped and shouted and laughed;
   And all the hills echoèd.

WILLIAM BLAKE

The Gardener

The gardener does not love to talk,
He makes me keep the gravel walk;
And when he puts his tools away,
He locks the door and takes the key.

Away behind the currant row
Where no one else but cook may go,
Far in the plots, I see him dig,
Old and serious, brown and big.

He digs the flowers, green, red, and blue,
Nor wishes to be spoken to.
He digs the flowers and cuts the hay,
And never seems to want to play.

Silly gardener! summer goes,
And winter comes with pinching toes,
When in the garden bare and brown
You must lay your barrow down.

Well now, and while the summer stays,
To profit by these garden days
O how much wiser you would be
To play at Indian wars with me!

ROBERT LOUIS STEVENSON

Go, *Lovely Rose*

Go, lovely Rose—
Tell her that wastes her time and me,
   That now she knows,
When I resemble her to thee,
How sweet and fair she seems to be.

   Tell her that's young,
And shuns to have her graces spied,
   That hadst thou sprung
In deserts where no men abide,
Thou must have uncommended died.

   Small is the worth
Of beauty from the light retired:
   Bid her come forth,
Suffer herself to be desired,
And not blush so to be admired.

   Then die—that she
The common fate of all things rare
   May read in thee;
How small a part of time they share
That are so wondrous sweet and fair!

EDMUND WALLER

"There Was a Little Girl"

There was a little girl, who had a little curl
  Right in the middle of her forehead,
And when she was good, she was very, very good
  But when she was bad she was horrid.

She stood on her head, on her little trundle-bed,
  With nobody by for to hinder;
She screamed and she squalled, she yelled and she bawled,
  And drummed her little heels against the winder.

Her mother heard the noise, and thought it was the boys
  Playing in the empty attic,
She rushed upstairs, and caught her unawares,
  And spanked her, most emphatic.

HENRY WADSWORTH LONGFELLOW

Aladdin

When I was a beggarly boy,
   And lived in a cellar damp,
I had not a friend nor a toy,
   But I had Aladdin's lamp;
When I could not sleep for the cold,
   I had fire enough in my brain,
And builded, with roofs of gold,
   My beautiful castles in Spain!

Since then I have toiled day and night,
   I have money and power good store,
But I'd give all my lamps of silver bright
   For the one that is mine no more.
Take, Fortune, whatever you choose;
   You gave, and may snatch again;
I have nothing 'twould pain me to lose,
   For I own no more castles in Spain!

JAMES RUSSELL LOWELL

Foreign Lands

Up into the cherry tree
Who should climb but little me?
I held the trunk with both my hands
And looked abroad on foreign lands.

I saw the next door garden lie,
Adorned with flowers, before my eye,
And many pleasant places more
That I had never seen before.

I saw the dimpling river pass
And be the sky's blue looking-glass;
The dusty roads go up and down
With people tramping in to town.

If I could find a higher tree,
Farther and farther I should see,
To where the grown-up river slips
Into the sea among the ships;

To where the roads on either hand
Lead onward into fairy land,
Where all the children dine at five,
And all the playthings come alive.

ROBERT LOUIS STEVENSON

Beware Fair Maid

Beware fair maid of musky courtiers' oaths,
Take heed what gifts and favors you receive,
Let not the fading gloss of silken clothes
Dazzle your virtue, or your fame bereave.
  For lose but once the hold you have of grace,
  Who'll e'er respect your fortune or your face?

Each greedy hand will strive to catch the flower
When none regards the stalk it grows upon,
Each creature seeks the fruit still to devour
But leave the tree to fall or stand alone.
  Yet this advice, fair creature, take of me,
  Let none take fruit, unless he take the tree.

Believe no oaths, nor much protesting men,
Credit no vows, nor no bewailing songs,
Let courtiers swear, forswear, and swear again;
Their hearts do live ten regions from their tongues.
  For when with oaths they make thy heart to tremble
  Believe them least, for then they most dissemble.

Beware lest Caesar do corrupt thy mind
Or fond Ambition sell thy modesty.
Say though a king thou ever courteous find
He cannot garden thy virginity.
  Begin with king, to subject you will fall,
  From lord to lackey, and at last to all.

AUTHOR UNKNOWN

Ballad of the Tempest

We were crowded in the cabin,
　　Not a soul would dare to sleep,—
It was midnight on the waters,
　　And a storm was on the deep.

'Tis a fearful thing in winter
　　To be shattered by the blast,
And to hear the rattling trumpet
　　Thunder, "Cut away the mast!"

So we shuddered there in silence,—
　　For the stoutest held his breath,
While the hungry sea was roaring
　　And the breakers talked with death.

As thus we sat in darkness,
　　Each one busy with his prayers,
"We are lost!" the captain shouted,
　　As he staggered down the stairs.

But his little daughter whispered,
　　As she took his icy hand,
"Isn't God upon the ocean,
　　Just the same as on the land?"

Then we kissed the little maiden,
　　And we spake in better cheer,
And we anchored safe in harbor
　　When the morn was shining clear.

JAMES THOMAS FIELDS

Child's Song

I have a garden of my own,
  Shining with flowers of every hue;
I loved it dearly while alone,
  But I shall love it more with you:
And there the golden bees shall come,
  In summer time at break of morn,
And wake us with their busy hum
  Around the Siha's fragrant thorn.
I have a fawn from Aden's land,
  On leafy buds and berries nursed;
And you shall feed him from your hand,
  Though he may start with fear at first,
And I will lead you where he lies
  For shelter in the noon-tide heat;
And you may touch his sleeping eyes,
  And feel his little silvery feet.

THOMAS MOORE

The Toys

My little son, who looked from thoughtful eyes
And moved and spoke in quiet grown-up wise,
Having my law the seventh time disobeyed,
I struck him, and dismissed
With hard words and unkissed,
—His mother, who was patient, being dead.
Then, fearing lest his grief should hinder sleep,
I visited his bed,
But found him slumbering deep,
With darkened eyelids, and their lashes yet
From his late sobbing wet.
And I, with moan,
Kissing away his tears, left others of my own;
For, on a table drawn beside his head,
He had put, within his reach,
A box of counters and a red-veined stone,
A piece of glass abraded by the beach,
And six or seven shells,
A bottle with bluebells,
And two French copper coins, ranged there with
        careful art,
To comfort his sad heart.
So when that night I prayed
To God, I wept, and said:
"Ah, when at last we lie with trancéd breath,
Not vexing Thee in death,
And Thou rememberest of what toys
We made our joys,
How weakly understood
Thy great commanded good,

Then, fatherly not less
Than I whom Thou hast molded from the clay,
Thou'lt leave Thy wrath, and say,
'I will be sorry for their childishness.'"

COVENTRY PATMORE

He little knew the sorrow that was in his vacant chair;
He never guessed they'd miss him, or he'd surely have
    been there;
He couldn't see his mother or the lump that filled her
    throat,
Or the tears that started falling as she read his hasty
    note;
And he couldn't see his father, sitting sorrowful and
    dumb,
Or he never would have written that he thought he
    couldn't come.
He little knew the gladness that his presence would
    have made,
And the joy it would have given, or he never would
    have stayed.
He didn't know how hungry had the little mother grown
Once again to see her baby and to claim him for her
    own.
He didn't guess the meaning of his visit Christmas Day
Or he never would have written that he couldn't get
    away.
He couldn't see the fading of the cheeks that once were
    pink,
And the silver in the tresses; and he didn't stop to think
How the years are passing swiftly, and next Christmas it
    might be
There would be no home to visit and no mother dear to
    see.
He didn't think about it—I'll not say he didn't care.
He was heedless and forgetful or he'd surely have been
    there.

Are you going home for Christmas? Have you written
   you'll be there?
Going home to kiss the mother and to show her that
   you care?
Going home to greet the father in a way to make him
   glad?
If you're not I hope there'll never come a time you'll
   wish you had.
Just sit down and write a letter—it will make their
   heartstrings hum
With a tune of perfect gladness—if you'll tell them
   that you'll come.

EDGAR GUEST

Where Did You Come From?

Where did you come from, Baby dear?
Out of the everywhere into here.

Where did you get your eyes so blue?
Out of the sky as I came through.

What makes the light in them sparkle and spin?
Some of the starry spikes left in.

Where did you get that little tear?
I found it waiting when I got here.

What makes your forehead so smooth and high?
A soft hand stroked it as I went by.

What makes your cheek like a warm white rose?
I saw something better than anyone knows.

Whence that three-corner'd smile of bliss?
Three angels gave me at once a kiss.

Where did you get this pearly ear?
God spoke, and it came out to hear.

Where did you get those arms and hands?
Love made itself into hooks and bands.

Feet, whence did you come, you darling things?
From the same box as the cherubs' wings.

How did they all come just to be you?
God thought of me, and so I grew.

But how did you come to us, you dear?
God thought of you, and so I am here.

GEORGE MACDONALD

Patty-Poem

She never puts her toys away;
Just leaves them scattered where they lay—
I try to scold her, and I say
   "You make me mad!"

But when to bed she has to chase,
The toys she left about the place
Remind me of her shining face,
   And make me glad.

When she grows up and gathers poise
I'll miss her harum-scarum noise,
And look in vain for scattered toys—
   And I'll be sad.

NICK KENNY

Making a Man

Hurry the baby as fast as you can,
Hurry him, worry him, make him a man.
Off with his baby clothes, get him in pants,
Feed him on brain foods and make him advance.
Hustle him, soon as he's able to walk,
Into a grammar school; cram him with talk.
Fill his poor head full of figures and facts,
Keep on a-jamming them in till it cracks.
Once boys grew up at a rational rate,
Now we develop a man while you wait,
Rush him through college, compel him to grab,
Of every known subject a dip and a dab.
Get him in business and after the cash,
All by the time he can grow a mustache
Let him forget he was ever a boy,
Make gold his god and its jingle his joy.
Keep him a-hustling and clear out of breath,
Until he wins—nervous prostration and death.

NIXON WATERMAN

To Youth

This I say to you:
Be arrogant! Be true!
True to April's lust that sings
Through your veins. These sharp Springs
Matter most . . . Afters years
Will be time enough to sleep . . .
Carefulness . . . and tears . . .

Now while life is raw and new,
Drink it clear, drink it deep!
Let the moonlight's lunacy
Tear away your cautions.
Be proud, and mad, and young, and free!
Grasp a comet! Kick at stars
Laughingly! Fight! Dare!
Arms are soft, breasts are white.
Magic's in the April night—

Never fear, Age will catch you,
Slow you down, ere it dispatch you
To your long and solemn quiet . . .
What will matter—then—the riot

Of the lilacs in the wind?
What will mean—then—the crush
Of lips at hours when birds hush?
Purple, green and flame will end
In a calm, gray blend.

Only graven in your soul
After all the rest is gone
There will be ecstasies . . .
These alone . . .

JOHN WEAVER

When I Was One-and-Twenty

When I was one-and-twenty
   I heard a wise man say,
"Give crowns and pounds and guineas
   But not your heart away;
Give pearls away and rubies
   But keep your fancy free."
But I was one-and-twenty,
   No use to talk to me.

When I was one-and-twenty
   I heard him say again,
"The heart out of the bosom
   Was never given in vain;
'Tis paid with sighs a-plenty
   And sold for endless rue."
And I am two-and-twenty,
   And oh, 'tis true, 'tis true.

A. E. HOUSMAN

How Old Are You?

Age is a quality of mind.
If you have left your dreams behind,
If hope is cold,
If you no longer look ahead,
If your ambitions' fires are dead—
Then you are old.

But if from life you take the best,
And if in life you keep the jest,
If love you hold;
No matter how the years go by,
No matter how the birthdays fly—
You are not old.

H.S. FRITSCH

Life

Daybreak

A Wind came up out of the sea,
And said, "O mists, make room for me."

It hailed the ships, and cried, "Sail on,
Ye mariners, the night is gone."

And hurried landward far away,
Crying, "Awake! it is the day."

It said unto the forest, "Shout!
Hang all your leafy banners out!"

It touched the wood-bird's folded wing,
And said, "O bird, awake and sing."

And o'er the farms, "O chanticleer,
Your clarion blow; the day is near."

It whispered to the fields of corn,
"Bow down, and hail the coming morn."

It shouted through the belfry tower,
"Awake, O bell! proclaim the hours."

It crossed the churchyard with a sigh,
And said, "Not yet! in quiet lie."

HENRY WADSWORTH LONGFELLOW

The Choice

Think thou and act; to-morrow thou shalt die.
  Outstretch'd in the sun's warmth upon the shore,
  Thou say'st: 'Man's measured path is all gone o'er:
Up all his years, steeply, with strain and sigh,
Man clomb until he touch'd the truth; and I,
  Even I, am he whom it was destined for.'
  How should this be? Art thou then so much more
Than they who sow'd, that thou shouldst reap thereby?

Nay, come up hither. From this wave-wash'd mound
  Unto the furthest flood-brim look with me;
Then reach on with thy thought till it be drown'd.
  Miles and miles distant though the last line be,
And though thy soul sail leagues and leagues beyond,—
  Still, leagues beyond those leagues, there is more sea.

DANTE GABRIEL ROSSETTI

The Power of Littles

Great events, we often find,
    On little things depend,
And very small beginnings
    Have oft a mighty end.

Letters joined make words,
    And words to books may grow,
As flake on flake descending
    Form an avalanche of snow.

A single utterance may good
    Or evil thought inspire;
One little spark enkindled
    May set a town on fire.

What volumes may be written
    With little drops of ink!
How small a leak, unnoticed,
    A mighty ship will sink!

A tiny insect's labor
    Makes the coral strand,
And mighty seas are girdled
    With grains of golden sand.

A daily penny, saved,
    A fortune may begin;
A daily penny, squandered,
    May lead to vice and sin.

Our life is made entirely
    Of moments multiplied,
As little streamlets, joining,
    Form the ocean's tide.

Our hours and days, our months and years,
    Are in small moments given:
They constitute our time below—
    Eternity in heaven.

ANONYMOUS

The Tide Rises, the Tide Falls

The tide rises, the tide falls,
The twilight darkens, the curfew calls;
Along the sea-sands damp and brown
The traveller hastens toward the town,
    And the tide rises, the tide falls.

Darkness settles on roofs and walls,
But the sea, the sea in the darkness calls;
The little waves, with their soft, white hands,
Efface the footprints in the sands,
    And the tide rises, the tide falls.

The morning breaks; the steeds in their stalls
Stamp and neigh, as the hostler calls;
The day returns, but nevermore
Returns the traveller to the shore,
    And the tide rises, the tide falls.

HENRY WADSWORTH LONGFELLOW

To His Coy Mistress

Had we but world enough, and time,
This coyness, lady, were no crime.
We would sit down, and think which way
To walk, and pass our long love's day.
Thou by the Indian Ganges' side
Shouldst rubies find: I by the tide
Of Humber would complain. I would
Love you ten years before the flood,
And you should, if you please, refuse
Till the conversion of the Jews;
My vegetable love should grow
Vaster than empires and more slow;
An hundred years should go to praise
Thine eyes, and on thy forehead gaze;
Two hundred to adore each breast,
But thirty thousand to the rest;
An age at least to every part,
And the last age should show your heart.
For, lady, you deserve this state;
Nor would I love at lower rate.

But at my back I always hear
Time's wingéd chariot hurrying near;
And yonder all before us lie
Deserts of vast eternity.
Thy beauty shall no more be found,
Nor in thy marble vault shall sound
My echoing song; then worms shall try
That long preserved virginity;
And your quaint honor turn to dust,

And into ashes all my lust:
The grave's a fine and private place,
But none, I think, do there embrace.

Now therefore, while the youthful hue
Sits on thy skin like morning dew,
And while thy willing soul transpires
At every pore with instant fires,
Now let us sport us while we may,
And now, like amorous birds of prey,
Rather at once our time devour
Than languish in his slow-chapped power,
Let us roll all our strength and all
Our sweetness up into one ball,
And tear our pleasures with rough strife
Thorough the iron gates of life:

Thus, though we cannot make our sun
Stand still, yet we will make him run.

ANDREW MARVELL

I Saw Two Clouds at Morning

I saw two clouds at morning,
 Tinged with the rising sun,
And in the dawn they floated on,
 And mingled into one:
I thought that morning cloud was blest,
It moved so sweetly to the west.

I saw two summer currents
 Flow smoothly to their meeting,
And join their course, with silent force,
 In peace each other greeting:
Calm was their course through banks of green,
While dimpling eddies played between.

Such be your gentle motion,
 Till life's last pulse shall beat;
Like summer's beam, and summer's stream,
 Float on, in joy, to meet
A calmer sea, where storms shall cease—
A purer sky, where all is peace.

JOHN GARDINER BRAINARD

Away with Funeral Music

Away with funeral music—set
　　The pipe to powerful lips—
The cup of life's for him that drinks
　　And not for him that sips.

ROBERT LOUIS STEVENSON

Time

> Time is
> Too slow for those who Wait,
> Too swift for those who Fear,
> Too long for those who Grieve,
> Too short for those who Rejoice;
> But for those who Love
> Time is
> Eternity.

ANONYMOUS

He Hears with Gladdened Heart the Thunder

He hears with gladdened heart the thunder
    Peal, and loves the falling dew;
He knows the earth above and under—
    Sits and is content to view.

He sits beside the dying ember,
    God for hope and man for friend,
Content to see, glad to remember,
    Expectant of the certain end.

ROBERT LOUIS STEVENSON

Gather Ye Roses

Gather ye roses while ye may,
    Old time is still a-flying;
A world where beauty fleets away
    Is no world for denying.
Come lads and lasses, fall to play
    Lose no more time in sighing.

The very flowers you pluck to-day
    To-morrow will be dying;
    And all the flowers are crying,
And all the leaves have tongues to say,—
Gather ye roses while ye may.

ROBERT LOUIS STEVENSON

Leisure

What is this life if, full of care,
We have no time to stand and stare.

No time to stand beneath the boughs
And stare as long as sheep or cows.

No time to see, when woods we pass,
Where squirrels hide their nuts in grass.

No time to see, in broad daylight,
Streams full of stars, like skies at night.

No time to turn at Beauty's glance,
And watch her feet, how they can dance.

No time to wait till her mouth can
Enrich that smile her eyes began.

A poor life this if, full of care,
We have no time to stand and stare.

WILLIAM HENRY DAVIES

A Bag of Tools

Isn't it strange
    That princes and kings,
And clowns that caper
    In sawdust rings,
And common people
    Like you and me
    Are builders for eternity?

Each is given a bag of tools,
    A shapeless mass,
A book of rules;
    And each must make—
Ere life is flown—
    A stumbling block
Or a steppingstone.

R. L. SHARPE

The Junk Box

My father often used to say:
"My boy don't throw a thing away:
You'll find a use for it some day."

So in a box he stored up things,
Bent nails, old washers, pipes and rings,
And bolts and nuts and rusty springs.

Despite each blemish and each flaw,
Some use for everything he saw;
With things material, this was law.

And often when he'd work to do,
He searched the junk box through and through
And found old stuff as good as new.

And I have often thought since then,
That father did the same with men;
He knew he'd need their help again.

It seems to me he understood
That men, as well as iron and wood,
May broken be and still be good.

Despite the vices he'd display
He never threw a man away,
But kept him for another day.

A human junk box is this earth
And into it we're tossed at birth,
To wait the day we'll be of worth.

Though bent and twisted, weak of will,
And full of flaws and lacking skill,
Some service each can render still.

EDGAR GUEST

The Ocean of Life

Ships that pass in the night, and speak each other in passing;
Only a signal shown and a distant voice in the darkness;
So in the ocean of life we pass and speak one another,
Only a look and a voice; then darkness again and a silence.

HENRY WADSWORTH LONGFELLOW

One Year to Live

If I had but one year to live;
One year to help; one year to give;
One year to love; one year to bless;
One year of better things to stress;
One year to sing; one year to smile;
To brighten earth a little while;
I think that I would spend each day,
In just the very self-same way
That I do now. For from afar
The call may come to cross the bar
At any time, and I must be
Prepared to meet eternity.
So if I have a year to live,
Or just a day in which to give
A pleasant smile, a helping hand,
A mind that tries to understand
A fellow-creature when in need,
'Tis one with me,—I take no heed;
But try to live each day He sends
To serve my gracious Master's ends.

MARY DAVIS REED

Take the World as It Is

Take the world as it is!—with its smiles and its sorrow,
    Its love and its friendship—its falsehood and truth—
Its schemes that depend on the breath of tomorrow!
    Its hopes which pass by like the dreams of our youth—
Yet, oh! whilst the light of affection may shine,
    The heart in itself hath a fountain of bliss!
In the *worst* there's some spark of a nature divine,
    And the wisest and best *take the world as it is*.

CHARLES SWAIN

Life Owes Me Nothing

Life owes me nothing. Let the years
Bring clouds or azure, joy or tears;
    Already a full cup I've quaffed;
    Already wept and loved and laughed,
And seen, in ever-endless ways,
New beauties overwhelm the days.

Life owes me nought. No pain that waits
Can steal the wealth from memory's gates;
    No aftermath of anguish slow
    Can quench the soul fire's early glow.
I breathe, exulting, each new breath,
Embracing Life, ignoring Death.

Life owes me nothing. One clear morn
Is boon enough for being born;
    And be it ninety years or ten,
    No need for me to question when.
While Life is mine, I'll find it good,
And greet each hour with gratitude.

ANONYMOUS

Song of the Lotos-Eaters

There is sweet music here that softer falls
Than petals from blown roses on the grass,
Or night-dews on still waters between walls
Of shadowy granite, in a gleaming pass;
Music that gentlier on the spirit lies,
Than tired eyelids upon tired eyes;
Music that brings sweet sleep down from the blissful skies.
Here are cool mosses deep,
And thro' the moss the ivies creep,
And in the stream the long-leaved flowers weep,
And from the craggy ledge the poppy hangs in sleep.

Why are we weigh'd upon with heaviness,
And utterly consumed with sharp distress,
While all things else have rest from weariness?
All things have rest: why should we toil alone,
We only toil, who are the first of things,
And make perpetual moan,
Still from one sorrow to another thrown:
Nor ever fold our wings,
And cease from wanderings,
Nor steep our brows in slumber's holy balm;
Nor harken what the inner spirit sings,
'There is no joy but calm!' —
Why should we only toil, the roof and crown of things?

Lo! in the middle of the wood,
The folded leaf is woo'd from out the bud
With winds upon the branch, and there
Grows green and broad, and takes no care,
Sun-steep'd at noon, and in the moon
Nightly dew-fed; and turning yellow
Falls, and floats adown the air.
Lo! sweeten'd with the summer light,
The full-juiced apple, waxing over-mellow,
Drops in a silent autumn night.
All its allotted length of days,
The flower ripens in its place,
Ripens and fades, and falls, and hath no toil,
Fast-rooted in the fruitful soil.

Hateful is the dark-blue sky,
Vaulted o'er the dark-blue sea.
Death is the end of life; ah, why
Should life all labour be?
Let us alone. Time driveth onward fast,
And in a little while our lips are dumb.
Let us alone. What is it that will last?
All things are taken from us, and become
Portions and parcels of the dreadful Past.
Let us alone. What pleasure can we have
To war with evil? Is there any peace
In ever climbing up the climbing wave?

All things have rest, and ripen toward the grave
In silence; ripen, fall and cease:
Give us long rest or death, dark death, or dreamful ease.

How sweet it were, hearing the downward stream,
With half-shut eyes ever to seem
Falling asleep in a half-dream!
To dream and dream, like yonder amber light,
Which will not leave the myrrh-bush on the height;
To hear each other's whisper'd speech;
Eating the Lotos day by day,
To watch the crisping ripples on the beach,
And tender curving lines of creamy spray;
To lend our hearts and spirits wholly
To the influence of mild-minded melancholy;
To muse and brood and live again in memory,
With those old faces of our infancy
Heap'd over with a mound of grass,
Two handfuls of white dust, shut in an urn of brass!

Dear is the memory of our wedded lives,
And dear the last embraces of our wives
And their warm tears: but all hath suffer'd change;
For surely now our household hearths are cold:
Our sons inherit us: our looks are strange:
And we should come like ghosts to trouble joy.

Or else the island princes over-bold
Have eat our substance, and the minstrel sings
Before them of the ten years' war in Troy,
And our great deeds, as half-forgotten things.
Is there confusion in the little isle?
Let what is broken so remain.
The Gods are hard to reconcile:
'Tis hard to settle order once again.
There *is* confusion worse than death,
Trouble on trouble, pain on pain,
Long labour unto aged breath,
Sore task to hearts worn out with many wars
And eyes grown dim with gazing on the pilot-stars.

But propt on beds of amaranth and moly,
How sweet (while warm airs lull us, blowing lowly)
With half-dropt eyelids still,
Beneath a heaven dark and holy,
To watch the long bright river drawing slowly
His waters from the purple hill—
To hear the dewy echoes calling
From cave to cave thro' the thick-twinèd vine—
To watch the emerald-colour'd water falling
Thro' many a wov'n acanthus-wreath divine!
Only to hear and see the far-off sparkling brine,
Only to hear were sweet, stretch'd out beneath the pine.

The Lotos blooms below the barren peak:
The Lotos blows by every winding creek:
All day the wind breathes low with mellower tone:
Thro' every hollow cave and alley lone
Round and round the spicy downs the yellow Lotos-dust is blown.
We have had enough of action, and of motion we,
Roll'd to starboard, roll'd to larboard, when the surge was
    seething free,
Where the wallowing monster spouted his foam-fountains
    in the sea.
Let us swear an oath, and keep it with an equal mind,
In the hollow Lotos-land to live and lie reclined
On the hills like Gods together, careless of mankind.
For they lie beside their nectar, and the bolts are hurl'd
Far below them in the valleys, and the clouds are lightly curl'd
Round their golden houses, girdled with the gleaming world:
Where they smile in secret, looking over wasted lands,
Blight and famine, plague and earthquake, roaring deeps
    and fiery sands,
Clanging fights, and flaming towns, and sinking ships,
    and praying hands.
But they smile, they find a music centred in a doleful song
Steaming up, a lamentation and an ancient tale of wrong,
Like a tale of little meaning tho' the words are strong;
Chanted from an ill-used race of men that cleave the soil,
Sow the seed, and reap the harvest with enduring toil,
Storing yearly little dues of wheat, and wine and oil;

Till they perish and they suffer—some, 'tis whisper'd—
    down in hell
Suffer endless anguish, others in Elysian valleys dwell,
Resting weary limbs at last on beds of asphodel.
Surely, surely, slumber is more sweet than toil, the shore
Than labour in the deep mid-ocean, wind and wave and oar;
O rest ye, brother mariners, we will not wander more.

ALFRED, LORD TENNYSON

You Never Can Tell

You never can tell when you send a word
  Like an arrow shot from a bow
By an archer blind, be it cruel or kind,
  Just where it may chance to go.
It may pierce the breast of your dearest friend,
  Tipped with its poison or balm,
To a stranger's heart in life's great mart
  It may carry its pain or its calm.

You never can tell when you do an act
  Just what the result will be,
But with every deed you are sowing a seed,
  Though the harvest you may not see.
Each kindly act is an acorn dropped
  In God's productive soil;
You may not know, but the tree shall grow
  With shelter for those who toil.

You never can tell what your thoughts will do
  In bringing you hate or love,
For thoughts are things, and their airy wings
  Are swifter than carrier doves.
They follow the law of the universe—
  Each thing must create its kind,
And they speed o'er the track to bring you back
  Whatever went out from your mind.

ELLA WHEELER WILCOX

My Mind to Me a Kingdom Is

My mind to me a kingdom is,
    Such present joys therein I find,
That it excels all other bliss
    That earth affords or grows by kind:
Though much I want which most would have,
Yet still my mind forbids to crave.

No princely pomp, no wealthy store,
    No force to win the victory,
No wily wit to salve a sore,
    No shape to feed a loving eye;
To none of these I yield as thrall:
For why? My mind doth serve for all.

I see how plenty [surfeits] oft,
    And hasty climbers soon do fall;
I see that those which are aloft
    Mishap doth threaten most of all;
They get with toil, they keep with fear:
Such cares my mind could never bear.

Content to live, this is my stay;
    I seek no more than may suffice;
I press to bear no haughty sway;
    Look, what I lack my mind supplies:
Lo, thus I triumph like a king,
Content with that my mind doth bring.

Some have too much, yet still do crave;
    I little have, and seek no more.
They are but poor, though much they have,
    And I am rich with little store;

They poor, I rich; they beg, I give;
They lack, I leave; they pine, I live.

I laugh not at another's loss;
    I grudge not at another's gain;
No worldly waves my mind can toss;
    My state at one doth still remain:
I fear no foe, I fawn no friend;
I loathe not life, nor dread my end.

Some weigh their pleasure by their lust,
    Their wisdom by their rage of will;
Their treasure is their only trust;
    A cloakèd craft their store of skill:
But all the pleasure that I find
Is to maintain a quiet mind.

My wealth is health and perfect ease;
    My conscience clear my chief defense;
I neither seek by bribes to please,
    Nor by deceit to breed offense:
Thus do I live; thus will I die;
Would all did so as well as I!

SIR EDWARD DYER

Commonplace

"A commonplace life," we say, and we sigh,
But why should we sigh as we say?
The commonplace sun in the commonplace sky
Makes up the commonplace day;
The moon and the stars are commonplace things,
And the flower that blooms, and the bird that sings,
But dark were the world, and sad our lot,
If the flowers failed, and the sun shone not;
And God, who studies each separate soul,
Out of commonplace lives makes His beautiful whole.

SUSAN COOLIDGE

If You Made Gentler the Churlish World

If you have spoken something beautiful,
Or touched the dead canvas to life,
Or made the cold stone to speak—
You who know the secret heart of beauty;
If you have done one thing
That has made gentler the churlish world,
Though mankind pass you by,
And feed and clothe you grudgingly—
Though the world starve you,
And God answer not your nightly prayers,
And you grow old hungering still at heart,
And walk friendless in your way,
And lie down at last forgotten—
If all this befall you who have created beauty,
You shall still leave a bequest to the world
Greater than institutions and riches and commerce;
And by the immutable law of the human heart
The God of the universe is your debtor,
If you have made gentler the churlish world.

MAX EHRMANN

Passion

Love's Philosophy

The fountains mingle with the river,
    And the rivers with the ocean;
The winds of heaven mix forever,
    With a sweet emotion;
Nothing in the world is single;
    All things by a law divine
In one another's being mingle:—
    Why not I with thine?

See! the mountains kiss high heaven,
    And the waves clasp one another;
No sister flower would be forgiven
    If it disdained its brother;
And the sunlight clasps the earth,
    And the moonbeams kiss the sea:—
What are all these kissings worth,
    If thou kiss not me?

PERCY BYSSHE SHELLEY

Midsummer

You loved me for a little,
    Who could not love me long;
You gave me wings of gladness
    And lent my spirit song.

You loved me for an hour
    But only with your eyes;
Your lips I could not capture
    By storm or by surprise.

Your mouth that I remember
    With rush of sudden pain
As one remembers starlight
    Or roses after rain . . .

Out of a world of laughter
    Suddenly I am sad. . . .
Day and night it haunts me,
    The kiss I never had.

SYDNEY KING RUSSELL

Bedouin Song

From the Desert I come to thee
    On a stallion shod with fire;
And the winds are left behind
    In the speed of my desire.
Under thy window I stand,
    And the midnight hears my cry:
I love thee, I love but thee,
    With a love that shall not die
        Till the sun grows cold,
        And the stars are old,
        And the leaves of the Judgment Book unfold!

Look from thy window and see
    My passion and my pain;
I lie on the sands below,
    And I faint in thy disdain.
Let the night-winds touch thy brow
    With the heat of my burning sigh,
And melt thee to hear the vow
    Of a love that shall not die
        Till the sun grows cold,
        And the stars are old,
        And the leaves of the Judgment Book unfold!

My steps are nightly driven,
    By the fever in my breast,
To hear from thy lattice breathed
    The word that shall give me rest.
Open the door of thy heart,
    And open thy chamber door,

And my kisses shall teach thy lips
   The love that shall fade no more
      Till the sun grows cold,
      And the stars are old,
      And the leaves of the Judgment Book unfold!

BAYARD TAYLOR

How Do I Love Thee?

How do I love thee? Let me count the ways.
　I love thee to the depth and breadth and height
　My soul can reach, when feeling out of sight
For the ends of Being and ideal Grace.
I love thee to the level of everyday's
　Most quiet need, by sun and candle-light.
　I love thee freely, as men strive for Right;
I love thee purely as they turn from Praise.

　I love thee with the passion put to use
In my old griefs, and with my childhood's faith.
　I love thee with a love I seemed to lose
With my lost saints,—I love thee with the breath,
　Smiles, tears, of all my life!—and, if God choose,
I shall but love thee better after death.

ELIZABETH BARRETT BROWNING

Why So Pale and Wan

Why so pale and wan, fond lover?
  Prithee, why so pale?
Will, when looking well can't move her,
  Looking ill prevail?
  Prithee, why so pale?

Why so dull and mute, young sinner?
  Prithee, why so mute?
Will, when speaking well can't win her,
  Saying nothing do 't?
  Prithee, why so mute?

Quit, quit for shame! This will not move;
  This cannot take her.
If of herself she will not love,
  Nothing can make her.
  The devil take her!

SIR JOHN SUCKLING

A Welcome

Come in the evening, or come in the morning,
Come when you're looked for, or come without warning,
Kisses and welcomes you'll find here before you,
And the oftener you come here the more I'll adore you.

THOMAS O. DAVIS

My Luve

O my luve is like a red, red rose,
    That's newly sprung in June:
O my luve is like the melodie,
    That's sweetly played in tune.

As fair art thou, my bonie lass,
    So deep in luve am I;
And I will luve thee still, my dear,
    Till a' the seas gang dry.

Till a' the seas gang dry, my dear,
    And the rocks melt wi' the sun:
And I will luve thee still, my dear,
    While the sands o' life shall run.

And fare thee weel, my only luve!
    And fare thee weel a while!
And I will come again, my luve,
    Tho' it were ten thousand mile.

ROBERT BURNS

When in Disgrace with Fortune and Men's Eyes

When, in disgrace with Fortune and men's eyes,
I all alone beweep my outcast state,
And trouble deaf heaven with my bootless cries,
And look upon myself and curse my fate,
Wishing me like to one more rich in hope,
Featured like him, like him with friends possessed,
Desiring this man's art, and that man's scope,
With what I most enjoy contented least;
Yet in these thoughts myself almost despising,
Haply I think on thee, and then my state,
Like to the lark at break of day arising
From sullen earth, sings hymns at heaven's gate;
    For thy sweet love remembered such wealth brings
    That then I scorn to change my state with kings.

WILLIAM SHAKESPEARE

All Paths Leads to You

All paths lead to you
    Where e'er I stray,
You are the evening star
    At the end of day.

All paths lead to you
    Hill-top or low,
You are the white birch
    In the sun's glow.

All paths lead to you
    Where e'er I roam.
You are the lark-song
    Calling me home!

BLANCHE SHOEMAKER WAGSTAFF

To—

One word is too often profaned
　　For me to profane it,
One feeling too falsely disdained
　　For thee to disdain it;
One hope is too like despair
　　For prudence to smother,
And pity from thee more dear
　　Than that from another.

I can give not what men call love,
　　But wilt thou accept not
The worship the heart lifts above
　　And the heavens reject not,—
The desire of the moth for the star,
　　Of the night for the morrow,
The devotion to something afar
　　From the sphere of our sorrow?

PERCY BYSSHE SHELLEY

When We Two Parted

When we two parted
   In silence and tears,
Half broken-hearted
   To sever for years,
Pale grew thy cheek and cold,
   Colder thy kiss;
Truly that hour foretold
   Sorrow to this.

In secret we met—
   In silence I grieve
That thy heart could forget,
   Thy spirit deceive.
If I should meet thee
   After long years,
How should I greet thee?—
   With silence and tears.

GEORGE GORDON, LORD BYRON

On Love

When love beckons to you, follow him,
Though his ways are hard and steep.
And when his wings enfold you yield to him.
Though the sword hidden among his pinions may wound you.
And when he speaks to you believe in him,
Though his voice may shatter your dreams as the north wind
    lays waste the garden.

For even as love crowns you so shall he crucify you.
    Even as he is for your growth so is he for your pruning.
Even as he ascends to your height and caresses your
    tenderest branches that quiver in the sun,
So shall he descend to your roots and shake them in
    their clinging to the earth.

Like sheaves of corn he gathers you unto himself.
He threshes you to make you naked.
He sifts you to free you from your husks.
He grinds you to whiteness.
He kneads you until you are pliant;
And then he assigns you to his sacred fire, that you may
    become sacred bread for God's sacred feast.

Love gives naught but itself and takes naught but from itself.
Love possesses not nor would it be possessed;
For love is sufficient unto love.

KAHLIL GIBRAN

Nightfall

I need so much the quiet of your love
After the day's loud strife;
I need your calm all other things above
After the stress of life.

I crave the haven that in your dear heart lies,
After all toil is done,
I need the star shine of your heavenly eyes,
After the day's great sun.

CHARLES HANSON TOWNE

What My Lover Said

By the merest chance, in the twilight gloom,
　In the orchard path he met me;
In the tall, wet grass, with its faint perfume,
And I tried to pass, but he made no room,
　Oh, I tried, but he would not let me.
So I stood and blushed till the grass grew red,
　With my face bent down above it,
While he took my hand as he whispering said—
(How the clover lifted each pink, sweet head,
To listen to all that my lover said;
　Oh, the clover in bloom, I love it!)

In the high, wet grass went the path to hide,
　And the low, wet leaves hung over;
But I could not pass upon either side,
For I found myself, when I vainly tried,
　In the arms of my steadfast lover.
And he held me there and he raised my head,
　While he closed the path before me,
And he looked down into my eyes and said—
(How the leaves bent down from the boughs o'er head,
To listen to all that my lover said;
　Oh, the leaves hanging lowly o'er me!)
Had he moved aside but a little way,
　I could surely then have passed him;
And he knew I never could wish to stay,
And would not have heard what he had to say,
　Could I only aside have cast him.
It was almost dark, and the moments sped,
　And the searching night wind found us,

But he drew me nearer and softly said—
(How the pure, sweet wind grew still, instead,
To listen to all that my lover said;
  Oh, the whispering wind around us!)

I know that the grass and the leaves will not tell,
  And I'm sure that the wind, precious rover,
Will carry my secret so safely and well
  That no being shall ever discover

One word of the many that rapidly fell
  From the soul-speaking lips of my lover;
    And from the moon and the stars that looked over
Shall never reveal what a fairy-like spell
They wove round about us that night in the dell,
  In the path through the dew-laden clover,
Nor echo the whispers that made my heart swell
  As they fell from the lips of my lover.

HOMER GREENE

The Night Has a Thousand Eyes

The night has a thousand eyes,
    And the day but one;
Yet the light of the bright world dies
    With the dying sun.

The mind has a thousand eyes,
    And the heart but one;
Yet the light of a whole life dies
    When love is done.

FRANCIS WILLIAM BOURDILLON

Delight in Disorder

A sweet disorder in the dress
Kindles in clothes a wantonness:
A lawn about the shoulders thrown
Into a fine distraction,
An erring lace, which here and there
Enthralls the crimson stomacher,
A cuff neglectful, and thereby
Ribbands to flow confusedly,
A winning wave (deserving note)
In the tempestuous petticoat,
A careless shoe-string, in whose tie
I see a wild civility,
Do more bewitch me, than when art
Is too precise in every part.

ROBERT HERRICK

Shall I Compare Thee to a Summer's Day?

Shall I compare thee to a summer's day?
Thou art more lovely and more temperate:
Rough winds do shake the darling buds of May,
And summer's lease hath all too short a date:
Sometime too hot the eye of heaven shines,
And often is his gold complexion dimm'd;
And every fair from fair sometime declines,
By chance, or nature's changing course untrimm'd;
But thy eternal summer shall not fade,
Nor lose possession of that fair thou ow'st,
Nor shall death brag thou wander'st in his shade,
When in eternal lines to time thou grow'st;
    So long as men can breathe, or eyes can see,
    So long lives this, and this gives life to thee.

WILLIAM SHAKESPEARE

My Love Is Like to Ice

My love is like to ice, and I to fire:
How comes it then that this her cold so great
Is not dissolved through my so hot desire,
But harder grows the more I her entreat?
Or how comes it that my exceeding heat
Is not allayed by her heart-frozen cold,
But that I burn much more in boiling sweat,
And feel my flames augmented manifold?
What more miraculous thing may be told,
That fire, which all things melts, should harden ice,
And ice, which is congealed with senseless cold,
Should kindle fire by wonderful device?
Such is the power of love in gentle mind,
That it can alter all the course of kind.

EDMUND SPENSER

Love

I love you,
Not only for what you are,
But for what I am
When I am with you.
I love you,
Not only for what
You have made of yourself,
But for what
You are making of me.

I love you
For the part of me
That you bring out;
I love you
For putting your hand
Into my heaped-up heart
And passing over
All the foolish, weak things
That you can't help
Dimly seeing there,
And for drawing out
Into the light
All the beautiful belongings
That no one else had looked
Quite far enough to find.
Winter's cold, or summer's heat,
Autumn's tempests, on it beat,
It can never know defeat,
    Never can rebel.

Such the love that I would gain,
Such the love, I tell thee plain,
Thou must give, or woo in vain;
    So to thee, farewell!
        Love me little, love me long,
        Is the burden of my song.

ANONYMOUS

She Walks in Beauty

She walks in beauty, like the night
Of cloudless climes and starry skies,
And all that's best of dark and bright
Meet in her aspect and her eyes;
Thus mellowed to that tender light
Which heaven to gaudy day denies.

One shade the more, one ray the less,
Had half impaired the nameless grace
Which waves in every raven tress
Or softly lightens o'er her face,
Where thoughts serenely sweet express
How pure, how dear their dwelling-place.

And on that cheek and o'er that brow
So soft, so calm, yet eloquent,
The smiles that win, the tints that glow
But tell of days in goodness spent,
A mind at peace with all below,
A heart whose love is innocent.

GEORGE GORDON, LORD BYRON

Appraisal

Never think she loves him wholly,
Never believe her love is blind,
All his faults are locked securely
In a closet of her mind;
All his indecisions folded
Like old flags that time has faded,
Limp and streaked with rain,
And his cautiousness like garments
Frayed and thin, with many a stain—
Let them be, oh, let them be,
There is treasure to outweigh them,
His proud will that sharply stirred,
Climbs as surely as the tide,
Senses strained too taut to sleep,
Gentleness to beast and bird,
Humor flickering hushed and wide
As the moon on moving water,
And a tenderness too deep
To be gathered in a word.

SARA TEASDALE

The Taxi

When I go away from you
The world beats dead
Like a slackened drum.
I call out for you against the jutted stars
And shout into the ridges of the wind.
Streets coming fast,
One after the other,
Wedge you away from me,
And the lamps of the city prick my eyes
So that I can no longer see your face.
Why should I leave you,
To wound myself upon the sharp edges of the night?

AMY LOWELL

If Thou Must Love Me

If thou must love me, let it be for naught
Except for love's sake only. Do not say,
"I love her for her smile—her look—her way
Of speaking gently,—for a trick of thought
That falls in well with mine, and certes brought
A sense of pleasant ease on such a day"—
For these things in themselves, Beloved, may
Be changed, or change for thee—and love, so wrought,
May be unwrought so. Neither love me for
Thine own dear pity's wiping my cheeks dry:
A creature might forget to weep, who bore
Thy comfort long, and lose thy love thereby!
But love me for love's sake, that evermore
Thou mayest love on, through love's eternity.

ELIZABETH BARRETT BROWNING

A Woman's Last Word

Let's contend no more, Love,
   Strive nor weep;
All be as before, Love,
   —Only sleep!

What so wild as words are?
   I and thou
In debate, as birds are,
   Hawk on bough!

See the creature stalking
   While we speak!
Hush and hide the talking,
   Cheek on cheek!

What so false as truth is,
   False to thee?
Where the serpent's tooth is
   Shun the tree—

Where the apple reddens
   Never pry—
Lest we lose our Edens,
   Eve and I.

Be a god and hold me
   With a charm!
Be a man and fold me
   With thine arm!

Teach me, only teach, Love!
     As I ought
I will speak thy speech, Love,
     Think thy thought—

Meet, if thou require it,
     Both demands,
Laying flesh and spirit
     In thy hands.

That shall be tomorrow
     Not tonight:
I must bury sorrow
     Out of sight:

—Must a little weep, Love,
     (Foolish me!)
And so fall asleep, Love,
     Loved by thee.

ROBERT BROWNING

To His Lute

My lute, awake! perform the last
Labour that thou and I shall waste,
    And end that I have now begun;
For when this song is said and past,
    My lute, be still, for I have done.

As to be heard where ear is none,
As lead to grave in marble stone,
    My song may pierce her heart as soon:
Should we then sing, or sigh, or moan?
    No, no, my lute! for I have done.

The rocks do not so cruelly
Repulse the waves continually,
    As she my suit and affection:
So that I am past remedy:
    Whereby my lute and I have done.

Proud of the spoil that thou hast got
Of simple hearts thorough Love's shot,
    By whom, unkind, thou hast them won;
Think not he hath his bow forgot,
    Although my lute and I have done.

Vengeance shall fall on thy disdain,
That makest but game of earnest pain:
    Trow not alone under the sun
Unquit to cause thy lover's plain,
    Although my lute and I have done.

May chance thee lie wither'd and old
The winter nights that are so cold,
    Plaining in vain unto the moon:
Thy wishes then dare not be told:
    Care then who list! for I have done.

And then may chance thee to repent
The time that thou has lost and spent
    To cause thy lover's sigh and swoon:
Then shalt thou know beauty but lent,
    And wish and want as I have done.

Now cease, my lute! this is the last
Labour that thou and I shall waste,
    And ended is that we begun:
Now is this song both sung and past—
    My lute, be still, for I have done.

SIR THOMAS WYATT

The Passionate Shepherd to His Love

Come live with me and be my love,
And we will all the pleasures prove
That hills and valleys, dales and fields,
And all the craggy mountains yields.

And we will sit upon the rocks
Seeing the shepherds feed their flocks,
By shallow rivers, to whose falls
Melodious birds sing madrigals.

And I will make thee beds of roses
And a thousand fragrant posies,
A cap of flowers, and a kirtle
Embroidered all with leaves of myrtle;

A gown made of the finest wool,
Which from our pretty lambs we pull;
Fair linéd slippers for the cold,
With buckles of the purest gold;

A belt of straw and ivy buds
With coral clasps and amber studs:
And if these pleasures may thee move,
Come live with me and be my love.

The shepherd swains shall dance and sing
For thy delight each May morning;
If these delights thy mind may move,
Then live with me and be my love.

CHRISTOPHER MARLOWE

Forgiven

You left me when the weary weight of sorrow
  Lay, like a stone, upon my bursting heart;
It seemed as if no shimmering tomorrow
  Could dry the tears that you had caused to start.
You left me, never telling why you wandered—
  Without a word, without a last caress;
Left me with but the love that I had squandered,
  The husks of love and a vast loneliness.

And yet if you came back with arms stretched toward
    me,
  Came back tonight, with carefree, smiling eyes,
And said: "My journeying has somehow bored me,
  And love, though broken, never, never dies!"
I would forget the wounded heart you gave me,
  I would forget the bruises on my soul.
My old-time gods would rise again to save me;
  My dreams would grow supremely new and whole.

What though youth lay, a tattered garment, o'er you?
  Warm words would leap upon my lips, long dumb;
If you came back, with arms stretched out before you,
  And told me, dear, that you were glad to come!

MARGARET E. SANGSTER

Go from Me

Go from me. Yet I feel that I shall stand
Henceforward in thy shadow. Nevermore
Alone upon the threshold of my door
Of individual life, I shall command
The uses of my soul, nor lift my hand
Serenely in the sunshine as before,
Without the sense of that which I forbore—
Thy touch upon the palm. The widest land
Doom takes to part us, leaves thy heart in mine
With pulses that beat double. What I do
And what I dream include thee, as the wine
Must taste of its own grapes. And when I sue
God for myself, He hears that name of thine,
And sees within my eyes the tears of two.

ELIZABETH BARRETT BROWNING

To My Dear and Loving Husband

If ever two were one, then surely we.
If ever man were loved by wife, then thee;
If ever wife was happy in a man,
Compare with me ye women if you can.
I prize thy love more than whole mines of gold,
Or all the riches that the East doth hold.
My love is such that rivers cannot quench,
Nor ought but love from thee give recompense.
Thy love is such I can no way repay;
The heavens reward thee manifold, I pray.
Then while we live, in love let's so persever,
That when we live no more we may live ever.

ANNE BRADSTREET

Let Me Not to the Marriage of True Minds

Let me not to the marriage of true minds
Admit impediments. Love is not love
Which alters when it alteration finds,
Or bends with the remover to remove:
O, no! it is an ever-fixed mark,
That looks on tempests and is never shaken;
It is the star to every wandering bark,
Whose worth's unknown, although his height be taken.
Love's not Time's fool, though rosy lips and cheeks
Within his bending sickle's compass come;
Love alters not with his brief hours and weeks,
But bears it out even to the edge of doom.
  If this be error, and upon me prov'd,
  I never writ, nor no man ever lov'd.

WILLIAM SHAKESPEARE

A Match

If love were what the rose is,
    And I were like the leaf,
Our lives would grow together
In sad or singing weather,
Blown fields or flowerful closes,
    Green pleasure or gray grief;
If love were what the rose is,
    And I were like the leaf.

If I were what the words are,
    And love were like the tune,
With double sound and single
Delight our lips would mingle,
With kisses glad as birds are
    That get sweet rain at noon;
If I were what the words are,
    And love were like the tune.

If you were life, my darling,
    And I, your love, were death,
We'd shine and snow together
Ere March made sweet the weather
With daffodil and starling
    And hours of fruitful breath;
If you were life, my darling,
    And I, your love, were death.

If you were thrall to sorrow,
    And I were page to joy,
We'd play for lives and seasons,

With loving looks and treasons,
And tears of night and morrow,
　And laughs of maid and boy;
If you were thrall to sorrow,
　And I were page to joy.

If you were April's lady,
　And I were lord in May,
We'd throw with leaves for hours,
And draw for days with flowers,
Till day like night were shady,
　And night were bright like day;
If you were April's lady,
　And I were lord in May.

If you were queen of pleasure,
　And I were king of pain,
We'd hunt down love together,
Pluck out his flying-feather,
And teach his feet a measure,
　And find his mouth a rein;
If you were queen of pleasure,
　And I were king of pain.

ALGERNON CHARLES SWINBURNE

To Althea, from Prison

When Love with unconfinèd wings
  Hovers within my gates,
And my divine Althea brings
  To whisper at the grates;
When I lie tangled in her hair
  And fetter'd to her eye,
The birds that wanton in the air
  Know no such liberty.

When flowing cups run swiftly round
  With no allaying Thames,
Our careless heads with roses bound,
  Our hearts with loyal flames;
When thirsty grief in wine we steep,
  When healths and draughts go free—
Fishes that tipple in the deep
  Know no such liberty.

When, like committed linnets, I
  With shriller throat shall sing
The sweetness, mercy, majesty,
  And glories of my King;
When I shall voice aloud how good
  He is, how great should be,
Enlargèd winds, that curl the flood,
  Know no such liberty.

Stone walls do not a prison make,
  Nor iron bars a cage;

Minds innocent and quiet take
  That for an hermitage;
If I have freedom in my love
  And in my soul am free,
Angels alone, that soar above,
  Enjoy such liberty.

RICHARD LOVELACE

Ode on a Grecian Urn

I

Thou still unravish'd bride of quietness.
  Thou foster-child of silence and slow time,
Sylvan historian, who canst thus express
  A flowery tale more sweetly than our rhyme:
What leaf-fring'd legend haunts about the shape
  Of deities or mortals, or of both,
    In Tempe or the dales of Arcady?
  What men or gods are these? What maidens loth?
What mad pursuit? What struggle to escape?
  What pipes and timbrels? What wild ecstasy?

II

Heard melodies are sweet, but those unheard
  Are sweeter; therefore, ye soft pipes, play on;
Not to the sensual ear, but, more endear'd,
  Pipe to the spirit ditties of no tone:
Fair youth, beneath the trees, thou canst not leave
  Thy song, nor ever can those trees be bare;
    Bold Lover, never, never canst thou kiss,
Though winning near the goal—yet, do not grieve;
  She cannot fade, though thou hast not thy bliss,
    For ever wilt thou love, and she be fair!
Ah, happy, happy boughs! that cannot shed
Your leaves, nor ever bid the Spring adieu;
And, happy melodist, unwearied,
  Forever piping songs forever new;

More happy love! more happy, happy love!
  Forever warm and still to be enjoy'd,
    Forever panting, and forever young;
All breathing human passion far above,
  That leaves a heart high-sorrowful and cloy'd,
    A burning forehead, and a parching tongue.

III

Who are these coming to the sacrifice?
  To what green altar, O mysterious priest,
Lead'st thou that heifer lowing at the skies,
  And all her silken flanks with garlands drest?
What little town by river or sea shore,
  Or mountain-built with peaceful citadel,
    Is emptied of this folk, this pious morn
And, little town, thy streets for evermore
  Will silent be; and not a soul to tell
    Why thou art desolate, can e'er return.

IV

O Attic shape! Fair attitude! with brede
  Of marble men and maidens overwrought,
With forest branches and the trodden weed;
    Thou, silent form, dost tease us out of thought
As doth eternity: Cold Pastoral!
  When old age shall this generation waste,

Thou shalt remain, in midst of other woe
Than ours, a friend to man, to whom thou say'st,
  'Beauty is truth, truth beauty,'—that is all
  Ye know on earth, and all ye need to know.

JOHN KEATS

When our two souls stand up erect and strong,
.Face to face, silent, drawing nigh and nigher,
Until the lengthening wings break into fire
At either curving point,—what bitter wrong
Can the earth do us, that we should not long
Be here contented? Think! In mounting higher,
The angels would press on us, and aspire
To drop some golden orb of perfect song
Into our deep, dear silence. Let us stay
Rather on earth, Belovèd—where the unfit
Contrarious moods of men recoil away
And isolate pure spirits, and permit
A place to stand and love in for a day,
With darkness and the death-hour rounding it.

ELIZABETH BARRETT BROWNING

At a Window

Give me hunger,
O you gods that sit and give
The world its orders.
Give me hunger, pain and want;
Shut me out with shame and failure
From your doors of gold and fame,
Give me your shabbiest, weariest hunger.
But leave me a little love;
A voice to speak to me in the day-end,
A hand to touch me in the dark room,
Breaking the long loneliness.
In the dusk of day-shapes,
Blurring the sunset,
One little wandering, western star
Thrust out from the changing shores of shadow.
Let me go to the window,
Watch there the day-shapes of dusk,
And wait and know the coming
Of a little love.

CARL SANDBURG

It Is Not Beauty I Demand

It is not Beauty I demand,
    A crystal brow, the moon's despair,
Nor the snow's daughter, a white hand,
    Nor mermaid's yellow pride of hair.

Tell me not of your starry eyes,
    Your lips that seem on roses fed,
Your breasts where Cupid trembling lies,
    Nor sleeps for kissing of his bed.

A bloomy pair of vermeil cheeks,
    Like Hebe's in her ruddiest hours,
A breath that softer music speaks
    Than summer winds a-wooing flowers.

These are but gauds; nay, what are lips?
    Coral beneath the ocean-stream,
Whose brink when your adventurer sips
    Full oft he perisheth on them.

And what are cheeks but ensigns oft
    That wave hot youth to fields of blood?
Did Helen's breast though ne'er so soft,
    Do Greece or Ilium any good?

Eyes can with baleful ardor burn,
    Poison can breath that erst perfumed,
There's many a white hand holds an urn
    With lovers' hearts to dust consumed.

For crystal brows—there's naught within,
    They are but empty cells for pride;
He who the Syren's hair would win
    Is mostly strangled in the tide.

Give me, instead of beauty's bust,
    A tender heart, a loyal mind,
Which with temptation I could trust.
    Yet never linked with error find.

One in whose gentle bosom I
    Could pour my secret heart of woes,
Like the care-burdened honey-fly
    That hides his murmurs in the rose.

My earthly comforter! whose love
    So indefeasible might be,
That when my spirit won above
    Hers could not stay for sympathy.

GEORGE DARLEY

For Love's Sake Only

If thou must love me, let it be for nought
Except for love's sake only. Do not say
"I love her for her smile—her look—her way
Of speaking gently,—for a trick of thought
That falls in well with mine, and certes brought
A sense of pleasant ease on such a day"—
For these things in themselves, Beloved, may
Be changed, or change for thee,—and love, so wrought,
May be unwrought so. Neither love me for
Thine own dear pity's wiping my cheeks dry,—
A creature might forget to weep, who bore
Thy comfort long, and lose thy love thereby!
But love me for love's sake, that evermore
Thou mayst love on, through love's eternity.

ELIZABETH BARRETT BROWNING

Need of Loving

Folk need a lot of loving in the morning;
 The day is all before, with cares beset—
The cares we know, and they that give no warning;
 For love is God's own antidote for fret.

Folk need a heap of loving at the noontime—
 In the battle lull, the moment snatched from strife—
Halfway between the waking and the croon time,
 While bickering and worriment are rife.

Folk hunger so for loving at the nighttime,
 When wearily they take them home to rest—
At slumber song and turning-out-the-light time—
 Of all the times for loving, that's the best.

Folk want a lot of loving every minute—
 The sympathy of others and their smile!
Till life's end, from the moment they begin it,
 Folks need a lot of loving all the while.

STRICKLAND GILLILAN

Summer Days

In summer, when the days were long,
We walked together in the wood:
 Our heart was light, our step was strong;
Sweet flutterings were there in our blood,
 In summer, when the days were long.

We strayed from morn till evening came;
We gathered flowers, and wove us crowns;
 We walked mid poppies red as flame,
Or sat upon the yellow downs;
 And always wished our life the same.

In summer, when the days were long,
We leaped the hedgerow, crossed the brook;
 And still her voice flowed forth in song,
Or else she read some graceful book,
 In summer, when the days were long.

And then we sat beneath the trees,
With shadows lessening in the noon;
 And in the sunlight and the breeze,
We feasted, many a gorgeous June,
 While larks were singing o'er the leas.

In summer, when the days were long,
On dainty chicken, snow-white bread.
 We feasted, with no grace but song;
We plucked wild strawb'rries, ripe and red,
 In summer, when the days were long.

We loved, and yet we knew it not,—
For loving seemed like breathing then;
　We found a heaven in every spot;
Saw angels, too, in all good men;
　And dreamed of God in grove and grot.

In summer, when the days are long,
Alone I wander, muse alone.
　I see her not; but that old song
Under the fragrant wind is blown,
　In summer, when the days are long.

Alone I wander in the wood:
But one fair spirit hears my sighs;
　And half I see, so glad and good,
The honest daylight of her eyes,
　That charmed me under earlier skies.

In summer, when the days are long,
I love her as we loved of old.
　My heart is light, my step is strong;
For love brings back those hours of gold,
　In summer, when the days are long.

AUTHOR UNKNOWN

Believe Me, If All Those
Endearing Young Charms

Believe me, if all those endearing young charms,
  Which I gaze on so fondly today,
Were to change by tomorrow, and fleet in my arms,
  Like fairy-gifts fading away,
Thou wouldst still be adored, as this moment thou art,
  Let thy loveliness fade as it will,
And around the dear ruin each wish of my heart
  Would entwine itself verdantly still.

It is not while beauty and youth are thine own,
  And thy cheeks unprofaned by a tear,
That the fervour and faith of a soul can be known,
  To which time will but make thee more dear;
No, the heart that has truly loved never forgets,
  But as truly loves on to the close,
As the sunflower turns on her god, when he sets,
  The same look which she turned when he rose.

THOMAS MOORE

I Love You

I love your lips when they're wet with wine
  And red with a wild desire;
I love your eyes when the lovelight lies
  Lit with a passionate fire.
I love your arms when the strands enmesh
  Your kisses against my face.

Not for me the cold, calm kiss
  Of a virgin's bloodless love;
Not for me the saint's white bliss,
  Nor the heart of a spotless dove.
But give me the love that so freely gives
  And laughs at the whole world's blame,
With your body so young and warm in my arms,
  It set my poor heart aflame.

So kiss me sweet with your warm wet mouth,
  Still fragrant with ruby wine,
And say with a fervor born of the South
  That your body and soul are mine.
Clasp me close in your warm young arms,
  While the pale stars shine above,
And we'll live our whole young lives away
  In the joys of a living love.

ELLA WHEELER WILCOX

Faithful to Thee, in My Fashion

Last night, ah, yesternight, betwixt her lips and mine
　There fell thy shadow, Cynara! thy breath was shed
Upon my soul between the kisses and the wine;
　And I was desolate and sick of an old passion,
　Yea, I was desolate and bowed my head:
　I have been faithful to thee, Cynara! in my fashion.

All night upon mine heart I felt her warm heart beat,
　Night-long within mine arms in love and sleep she lay;
Surely the kisses of her bought red mouth were sweet;
　But I was desolate and sick of an old passion,
　When I awoke and found the dawn was gray:
　I have been faithful to thee, Cynara! in my fashion.

I have forgot much, Cynara! gone with the wind,
　Flung roses, roses riotously with the throng,
Dancing, to put thy pale, lost lilies out of mind;
　But I was desolate and sick of an old passion,
　Yea, all the time, because the dance was long:
　I have been faithful to thee, Cynara! in my fashion.

I cried for madder music and for stronger wine,
　But when the feast is finished and the lamps expire,
Then falls thy shadow, Cynara! the night is thine;
　And I am desolate and sick of an old passion,
　Yea, hungry for the lips of my desire:
　I have been faithful to thee, Cynara! in my fashion.

ERNEST DOWSON

She Was a Phantom of Delight

She was a phantom of delight
When first she gleamed upon my sight;
A lovely apparition, sent
To be a moment's ornament;
Her eyes as stars of twilight fair;
Like twilight's, too, her dusky hair;
But all things else about her drawn
From May-time and the cheerful dawn;
A dancing shape, an image gay,
To haunt, to startle and waylay.

I saw her upon nearer view,
A Spirit, yet a Woman too!
Her household motions light and free,
And steps of virgin liberty;
A countenance in which did meet
Sweet records, promises as sweet;
A creature not too bright or good
For human nature's daily food;
For transient sorrows, simple wiles,
Praise, blame, love, kisses, tears, and smiles.

And now I see with eye serene
The very pulse of the machine;
A being breathing thoughtful breath,
A traveller between life and death;
The reason firm, the temperate will,
Endurance, foresight, strength, and skill;
A perfect Woman, nobly planned,
To warn, to comfort, and command;

And yet a Spirit still, and bright
With something of angelic light.

WILLIAM WORDSWORTH

Together

You and I by this lamp with these
Few books shut out the world. Our knees
Touch almost in this little space.
But I am glad. I see your face.
The silences are long, but each
Hears the other without speech.
And in this simple scene there is
The essence of all subtleties,
The freedom from all fret and smart,
The one sure sabbath of the heart.

The world—we cannot conquer it,
Nor change the minds of fools one whit.
Here, here alone do we create
Beauty and peace inviolate;
Here night by night and hour by hour
We build a high impregnable tower
Whence may shine, now and again,
A light to light the feet of men
When they see the rays thereof:
And this is marriage, this is love.

LUDWIG LEWISOHN

On Marriage

You were born together, and together you shall be
    forevermore.
You shall be together when the white wings of death
    scatter your days.
Ay, you shall be together even in the silent memory
    of God.
But let there be spaces in your togetherness,
And let the winds of the heavens dance between you.

Love one another, but make not a bond of love:
Let it rather be a moving sea between the shores
    of your souls.
Fill each other's cup but drink not from one cup.
Give one another of your bread but eat not from
    the same loaf.
Sing and dance together and be joyous, but let each
    one of you be alone,
Even as the strings of a lute are alone though they quiver
    with the same music.

Give your hearts, but not into each other's keeping.
For only the hand of Life can contain your hearts.
And stand together yet not too near together:
For the pillars of the temple stand apart,
And the oak tree and the cypress grow not in each
    other's shadow.

KAHLIL GIBRAN

The Indian Serenade

I arise from dreams of thee
In the first sweet sleep of night,
When the winds are breathing low,
And the stars are shining bright
I arise from dreams of thee,
And a spirit in my feet
Hath led me—who knows how?
To thy chamber window, Sweet!

The wandering airs they faint
On the dark, the silent stream—
The champak odors fail
Like sweet thoughts in a dream;
The nightingale's complaint,
It dies upon her heart;
As I must on thine,
Oh, beloved as thou art!

O lift me from the grass!
I die! I faint! I fail!
Let thy love in kisses rain
On my lips and eyelids pale.
My cheek is cold and white, alas!
My heart beats loud and fast;—
Oh! press it to thine own again,
Where it will break at last.

PERCY BYSSHE SHELLEY

The Legacy

When last I died, and, dear, I die
  As often as from thee I go,
  Though it be but an hour ago
—And lovers' hours be full eternity—
I can remember yet, that I
  Something did say, and something did bestow;
Though I be dead, which sent me, I might be
Mine own executor, and legacy.

I heard me say, "Tell her anon,
  That myself," that is you, not I,
  "Did kill me," and when I felt me die,
I bid me send my heart, when I was gone;
But I alas! could there find none;
  When I had ripp'd, and search'd where hearts
    should be
It kill'd me again, that I who still was true
In life, in my last will should cozen you.

Yet I found something like a heart,
  But colors it and corners had;
  It was not good, it was not bad,
It was entire to none, and few had part;
As good as could be made by art
  It seemed, and therefore for our loss be sad.
I meant to send that heart instead of mine,
But O! no man could hold it, for 'twas thine.

JOHN DONNE

My True Love Hath My Heart . . .

My true love hath my heart, and I have his,
By just exchange one for the other given.
I hold his dear, and mine he cannot miss;
There never was a better bargain driven.
His heart in me keeps me and him in one;
My heart in him his thoughts and senses guides;
He loves my heart, for once it was his own;
I cherish his, because in me it bides.
His heart his wound receivéd from my sight;
My heart was wounded with his wounded heart;
For as from me on him his hurt did light
So still methought in me his hurt did smart:
Both equal hurt, in this change sought our bliss;
My true love hath my heart, and I have his.

SIR PHILIP SIDNEY

Friendship

From Devotions XVII

No man is an island, entire of itself;
every man is a piece of the continent,
    a part of the main;
. . . any man's death diminishes me, because
I am involved in mankind;
and therefore never send to know for whom the bell
    tolls; it tolls for thee.

JOHN DONNE

On Friendship

And let your best be for your friend.
If he must know the ebb of your tide,
    let him know its flood also.
For what is your friend that you should seek him
    with hours to kill?
Seek him always with hours to live.
For it is his to fill your need, but not your emptiness.
And in the sweetness of friendship let there be
    laughter, and sharing of pleasures.
For in the dew of little things the heart finds its
    morning and is refreshed.

Your friend is your needs answered.
He is your field which you sow with love
    and reap with thanksgiving.
And he is your board and your fireside.
For you come to him with your hunger,
    and you seek him for peace.

KAHLIL GIBRAN

Who Are My People?

My people? Who are they?
I went into the church where the congregation
Worshipped my God. Were they my people?
I felt no kinship to them as they knelt there.
My people! Where are they?
I went into the land where I was born,
Where men spoke my language . . .
I was a stranger there.
"My people," my soul cried. "Who are my people?"

Last night in the rain I met an old man
Who spoke a language I do not speak,
Which marked him as one who does not know my God.
With apologetic smile he offered me
The shelter of his patched umbrella.
I met his eyes . . . And then I knew . . . .

ROSA ZAGNONI MARINONI

The Human Touch

'Tis the human touch in this world that counts,
   The touch of your hand and mine,
Which means far more to the fainting heart
   Than shelter and bread and wine;
For shelter is gone when the night is o'er,
   And bread lasts only a day,
But the touch of the hand and the sound of the voice
   Sing on in the soul alway.

SPENCER MICHAEL FREE

Plea for Tolerance

If we but knew what forces helped to mold
  The lives of others from their earliest years—
  Knew something of their background, joys and tears,
And whether or not their youth was drear and cold,
Or if some dark belief had taken hold
  And kept them shackled, torn with doubts and fears
  So long it crushed the force that perseveres
And made their hearts grow prematurely old,—

Then we might judge with wiser, kindlier sight,
  And learn to put aside our pride and scorn . . .
Perhaps no one can ever quite undo
  His faults or wholly banish some past blight—
The tolerant mind is purified, reborn,
  And lifted upward to a saner view.

MARGARET E. BRUNER

To Know All Is to Forgive All

If I knew you and you knew me—
If both of us could clearly see,
And with an inner sight divine
The meaning of your heart and mine—
I'm sure that we would differ less
And clasp our hands in friendliness;
Our thoughts would pleasantly agree
If I knew you, and you knew me.

If I knew you and you knew me,
As each one knows his own self, we
Could look each other in the face
And see therein a truer grace.

Life has so many hidden woes,
So many thorns for every rose;
The "why" of things our hearts would see,
If I knew you and you knew me.

NIXON WATERMAN

My Playmate

The pines were dark on Ramoth hill,
    Their song was soft and low;
The blossoms in the sweet May wind
    Were falling like the snow.

The blossoms drifted at our feet,
    The orchard birds sang clear;
The sweetest and the saddest day
    It seemed of all the year.

For, more to me than birds or flowers,
    My playmate left her home.
And took with her the laughing spring,
    The music and the bloom.

She kissed the lips of kith and kin,
    She laid her hand in mine:
What more could ask the bashful boy
    Who fed her father's kine?

She left us in the bloom of May:
    The constant years told o'er
Their seasons with as sweet May morns,
    But she came back no more.

I walk, with noiseless feet, the round
    Of uneventful years;
Still o'er and o'er I sow the spring
    And reap the autumn ears.

She lives where all the golden year
    Her summer roses blow;
The dusky children of the sun
    Before her come and go.

There haply with her jewelled hands
    She smooths her silken gown,—
No more the homespun lap wherein
    I shook the walnuts down.

The wild grapes wait us by the brook,
    The brown nuts on the hill,
And still the May-day flowers make sweet
    The woods of Follymill.

The lilies blossom in the pond,
    The bird builds in the tree,
The dark pines sing on Ramoth hill
    The slow song of the sea.

I wonder if she thinks of them,
    And how the old time seems,—
If ever the pines of Ramoth wood
    Are sounding in her dreams.

I see her face, I hear her voice;
    Does she remember mine?
And what to her is now the boy
    Who fed her father's kine?

What cares she that the orioles build
    For other eyes than ours,—
That other hands with nuts are filled,
    And other laps with flowers?

O playmate in the golden time!
    Our mossy seat is green,
Its fringing violets blossom yet,
    The old trees o'er it lean.

The winds so sweet with birch and fern
    A sweeter memory blow;
And there in spring the veeries sing
    The song of long ago.

And still the pines of Ramoth wood
    Are moaning like the sea,—
The moaning of the sea of change
    Between myself and thee!

JOHN GREENLEAF WHITTIER

There Is Always a Place for You

There is always a place for you at my table,
　　You never need to be invited.
I'll share every crust as long as I'm able,
　　And know you will be delighted.
There is always a place for you by my fire,
　　And though it may burn to embers,
If warmth and good cheer are your desire
　　The friend of your heart remembers!
There is always a place for you by my side,
　　And should the years tear us apart,
I will face lonely moments more satisfied
　　With a place for you in my heart!

ANNE CAMPBELL

God Bless You

I seek in prayerful words, dear friend,
　　My heart's true wish to send you,
That you may know that, far or near,
　　My loving thoughts attend you.

I cannot find a truer word,
　　Nor better to address you;
Nor song, nor poem have I heard
　　Is sweeter than God bless you!

God bless you! So I've wished you all
　　Of brightness life possesses;
For can there any joy at all
　　Be yours unless God blesses?

God bless you! So I breathe a charm
　　Lest grief's dark night oppress you,
For how can sorrow bring you harm
　　If 'tis God's way to bless you?

And so, "through all thy days
　　May shadows touch thee never—"
But this alone—God bless thee—
　　Then art thou safe forever.

ANONYMOUS

Forbearance

Hast thou named all the birds without a gun?
Loved the wood-rose, and left it on its stalk?
At rich men's tables eaten bread and pulse?
Unarmed, faced danger with a heart of trust?
And loved so well a high behavior,
In man or maid, that thou from speech refrained,
Nobility more nobly to repay?
O, be my friend, and teach me to be thine!

RALPH WALDO EMERSON

Accept My Full Heart's Thanks

Your words came just when needed.
Like a breeze,
Blowing and bringing from the wide salt sea
Some cooling spray, to meadow scorched with heat
And choked with dust and clouds of sifted sand
That hateful whirlwinds, envious of its bloom,
Had tossed upon it. But the cool sea breeze
Came laden with the odors of the sea
And damp with spray, that laid the dust and sand
And brought new life and strength to blade and bloom
So words of thine came over miles to me,
Fresh from the mighty sea, a true friend's heart,
And brought me hope, and strength, and swept away
The dusty webs that human spiders spun
Across my path. Friend—and the word means much—
So few there are who reach like thee, a hand
Up over all the barking curs of spite
And give the clasp, when most its need is felt,
Friend, newly found, accept my full heart's thanks.

ELLA WHEELER WILCOX

New Friends and Old Friends

Make new friends, but keep the old;
Those are silver, these are gold.
New-made friendships, like new wine,
Age will mellow and refine.
Friendships that have stood the test—
Time and change—are surely best;
Brow may wrinkle, hair grow gray;
Friendship never knows decay.
For 'mid old friends, tried and true,
Once more we our youth renew.
But old friends, alas! may die;
New friends must their place supply.
Cherish friendship in your breast—
New is good, but old is best;
Make new friends, but keep the old;
Those are silver, these are gold.

JOSEPH PARRY

Friendship Is Love without His Wings

Why should my anxious breast repine,
    Because my youth is fled?
Days of delight may still be mine;
    Affection is not dead.
In tracing back the years of youth,
One firm record, one lasting truth
    Celestial consolation brings;
Bear it, ye breezes, to the seat
Where first my heart responsive beat,—
    "Friendship is Love without his wings!"

GEORGE GORDON, LORD BYRON

A Poison Tree

I was angry with my friend;
I told my wrath, my wrath did end.
I was angry with my foe:
I told it not, my wrath did grow.

And I watered it in fears
Night and morning with my tears,
And I sunned it with smiles
And with soft deceitful wiles.

And it grew both day and night,
Till it bore an apple bright,
And my foe beheld it shine,
And he knew that it was mine—

And into my garden stole
When the night had veiled the pole;
In the morning, glad, I see
My foe outstretched beneath the tree.

WILLIAM BLAKE

Broken Friendship

Alas! they had been friends in youth,
But whispering tongues can poison truth!
And constancy lives in realms above!
And life is thorny, and Youth is vain!
And to be wroth with one we love,
Doth work like madness in the brain!
They parted—ne'er to meet again!
But never either found another
To free the hollow heart from paining!
They stood aloof, the scars remaining;
Like cliffs which had been rent asunder!
A dreary sea now flows between;
But neither heat, nor frost, nor thunder,
Shall wholly do away, I ween,
The marks of that which once had been.

SAMUEL TAYLOR COLERIDGE

The House by the Side of the Road

There are hermit souls that live withdrawn
  In the place of their self-content;
There are souls like stars, that dwell apart,
  In a fellowless firmament;
There are pioneer souls that blaze their paths
  Where highways never ran—
But let me live by the side of the road
  And be a friend to man.

Let me live in a house by the side of the road
  Where the race of men go by—
The men who are good and the men who are bad,
  As good and as bad as I.
I would not sit in the scorner's seat
  Or hurl the cynic's ban—
Let me live in a house by the side of the road
  And be a friend to man.

I see from my house by the side of the road,
  By the side of the highway of life,
The men who press with the ardor of hope,
  The men who are faint with the strife,
But I turn not away from their smiles nor their tears.
  Both parts of an infinite plan—
Let me live in a house by the side of the road
  And be a friend to man.

I know there are brook-gladdened meadows ahead,
  And mountains of wearisome height;

That the road passes on through the long afternoon
  And stretches away to the night.
And still I rejoice when the travelers rejoice
  And weep with the strangers that moan,
Nor live in my house by the side of the road
  Like a man who dwells alone.

Let me live in my house by the side of the road,
  It's here the race of men go by—
They are good, they are bad, they are weak,
  they are strong,
  Wise, foolish—so am I.
Then why should I sit in the scorner's seat,
  Or hurl the cynic's ban?
Let me live in my house by the side of the road
  And be a friend to man.

SAM WALTER FOSS

Around the Corner

Around the corner I have a friend,
In this great city that has no end;
Yet days go by, and weeks rush on,
And before I know it a year is gone,
And I never see my old friend's face,
For Life is a swift and terrible race.
He knows I like him just as well
As in the days when I rang his bell
And he rang mine. We were younger then,
And now we are busy, tired men:
Tired with trying to make a name.
"Tomorrow," I say, "I will call on Jim,
Just to show that I'm thinking of him."

But tomorrow comes—and tomorrow goes,
And the distance between us grows and grows
Around the corner! —yet miles away. . . .
"Here's a telegram, sir. . . ."
    "Jim died today."
And that's what we get, and deserve in the end:
Around the corner, a vanished friend.

CHARLES HANSON TOWNE

To My Friend

I have never been rich before,
　　But you have poured
Into my heart's high door
　　A golden hoard.

My wealth is the vision shared,
　　The sympathy,
The feast of the soul prepared
　　By you for me.

Together we wander through
　　The wooded ways.
Old beauties are green and new
　　Seen through your gaze.

I look for no greater prize
　　Than your soft voice.
The steadiness of your eyes
　　Is my heart's choice.

I have never been rich before,
　　But I divine
Your step on my sunlit floor
　　And wealth is mine!

ANNE CAMPBELL

I'm Nobody! Who Are You?

I'm Nobody! Who are you?
Are you—Nobody—Too?
Then there's a pair of us?
Don't tell! they'd advertise—you know!

How dreary—to be—Somebody!
How public—like a Frog—
To tell one's name—the livelong June—
To an admiring Bog!

EMILY DICKINSON

Character

The Inner Man

Beauty depends on simplicity—I mean the true simplicity
of a rightly and nobly ordered mind and character.
He is a fool who seriously inclines to weigh the beautiful
by any other standard than that of the good.
The good is the beautiful.
Grant me to be beautiful in the inner man.

PLATO

With Every Rising of the Sun

With every rising of the sun
Think of your life as just begun.

The past has shrived and buried deep
All yesterdays—there let them sleep . . . .

Concern yourself with but today,
Woo it and teach it to obey,

Your wish and will. Since time began
Today has been the friend of man . . . .

You and today! a soul sublime
And the great pregnant hour of time.

With God between to bind the twain—
Go forth I say—attain—attain.

ELLA WHEELER WILCOX

We are the music-makers,
    And we are the dreamers of dreams,
Wandering by lone sea-breakers,
    And sitting by desolate streams;
World-losers and world-forsakers,
    On whom the pale moon gleams:
Yet we are the movers and shakers
    Of the world for ever, it seems.

With wonderful deathless ditties
We build up the world's cities,
    And out of a fabulous story
    We fashion an empire's glory:
One man with a dream, at pleasure,
    Shall go forth and conquer a crown;
And three with a new song's measure
    Can trample an empire down.

We, in the ages lying
    In the buried past of the earth,
Built Nineveh with our sighing,
    And Babel itself with our mirth;

And o'erthrew them with prophesying
    To the old of the new world's worth;
For each age is a dream that is dying,
    Or one that is coming to birth.

ARTHUR O'SHAUGHNESSY

Ode to Solitude

Happy the man, whose wish and care
    A few paternal acres bound,
Content to breathe his native air,
        In his own ground.

Whose herds with milk, whose fields with bread,
    Whose flocks supply him with attire;
Whose trees in summer yield him shade,
        In winter, fire.

Blest who can unconcern'dly find
    Hours, days, and years slide soft away
In health of body, peace of mind,
        Quiet by day,

Sound sleep by night; study and ease
    Together mixt; sweet recreation,
And Innocence, which most does please
        With meditation.

Thus let me live, unseen, unknown;
    Thus unlamented let me die;
Steal from the world, and not a stone
        Tell where I lie.

ALEXANDER POPE

A Psalm of Life

Tell me not, in mournful numbers,
    Life is but an empty dream!—
For the soul is dead that slumbers,
    And things are not what they seem.

Life is real! Life is earnest!
    And the grave is not its goal;
Dust thou art, to dust returnest,
    Was not spoken of the soul.

Not enjoyment, and not sorrow,
    Is our destined end or way;
But to act, that each to-morrow
    Finds us farther than to-day.

Art is long, and Time is fleeting,
    And our hearts, though stout and brave,
Still, like muffled drums, are beating
    Funeral marches to the grave.

In the world's broad field of battle,
    In the bivouac of Life,

Be not like dumb, driven cattle!
    Be a hero in the strife!

Trust no Future, howe'er pleasant!
    Let the dead Past bury its dead!
Act,—act in the living Present!
    Heart within, and God o'erhead!

Lives of great men all remind us
    We can make our lives sublime,
And, departing, leave behind us
    Footprints on the sands of time;

Footprints, that perhaps another,
    Sailing o'er life's solemn main,
A forlorn and shipwrecked brother,
    Seeing, shall take heart again.

Let us, then, be up and doing,
    With a heart for any fate;
Still achieving, still pursuing,
    Learn to labor and to wait.

HENRY WADSWORTH LONGFELLOW

We Never Know How High We Are

We never know how high we are
Till we are asked to rise
And then if we are true to plan
Our statures touch the skies—

The Heroism we recite
Would be a normal thing
Did not ourselves the Cubits warp
For fear to be a King—

EMILY DICKINSON

The Noble Nature

It is not growing like a tree
    In bulk, doth make man better be;
Or standing long an oak, three hundred year,
To fall a log at last, dry, bald, and sear:
    A lily of a day
    Is fairer far in May,
  Although it fall and die that night,—
  It was the plant and flower of Light.
In small proportions we just beauties see,
And in short measures life may perfect be.

BEN JONSON

Count That Day Lost

If you sit down at set of sun
And count the acts that you have done,
    And, counting, find
One self-denying deed, one word
That eased the heart of him who heard,
    One glance most kind
That fell like sunshine where it went—
Then you may count that day well spent.

But if, through all the livelong day,
You've cheered no heart, by yea or nay—
    If, through it all
You've nothing done that you can trace
That brought the sunshine to one face—
    No act most small
That helped some soul and nothing cost—
Then count that day as worse than lost.

GEORGE ELIOT

The World Is Too Much with Us

The world is too much with us; late and soon,
Getting and spending, we lay waste our powers:
Little we see in Nature that is ours;
We have given our hearts away, a sordid boon!
The sea that bares her bosom to the moon;
The winds that will be howling at all hours,
And are up-gathered now like sleeping flowers;
For this, for everything, we are out of tune;
It moves us not.—Great God! I'd rather be
A pagan suckled in a creed outworn.
So might I, standing on this pleasant lea,
Have glimpses that would make me less forlorn;
Have sight of Proteus rising from the sea;
Or hear old Triton blow his wreathed horn.

WILLIAM WORDSWORTH

Money

When I had money, money, O!
 I knew no joy till I went poor;
For many a false man as a friend
 Came knocking all day at my door.

Then felt I like a child that holds
 A trumpet that he must not blow
Because a man is dead; I dared
 Not speak to let this false world know.

Much have I thought of life, and seen
 How poor men's hearts are ever light;
And how their wives do hum like bees
 About their work from morn till night.

So, when I hear these poor ones laugh,
 And see the rich ones coldly frown—
Poor men, think I, need not go up
 So much as rich men should come down.

When I had money, money, O!
 My many friends proved all untrue;
But now I have no money, O!
 My friends are real, though very few.

WILLIAM HENRY DAVIES

We Will Speak Out

We will speak out, we will be heard,
　　Though all earth's systems crack;
We will not bate a single word,
　　Nor take a letter back.
Let liars fear, let cowards shrink,
　　Let traitors turn away;
Whatever we have dared to think
　　That dare we also say.
We speak the truth, and what care we
　　For hissing and for scorn,
While some faint gleamings we can see
　　Of Freedom's coming morn?

JAMES RUSSELL LOWELL

Ozymandias

I met a traveler from an antique land,
Who said: Two vast and trunkless legs of stone
Stand in the desert. Near them, on the sand,
Half sunk, a shattered visage lies, whose frown,
And wrinkled lip, and sneer of cold command,
Tell that its sculptor well those passions read,
Which yet survive, stamped on these lifeless things,
The hand that mocked them, and the heart that fed:
And on the pedestal these words appear:
"My name is Ozymandias, King of Kings:
Look on my works, ye Mighty, and despair!"
Nothing beside remains. Round the decay
Of that colossal wreck, boundless and bare
The lone and level sands stretch far away.

PERCY BYSSHE SHELLEY

Don't Give Up

'Twixt failure and success the point's so fine
Men sometimes know not when they touch the line,
Just when the pearl was waiting one more plunge,
How many a struggler has thrown up the sponge!
Then take this honey from the bitterest cup:
"There is no failure save in giving up!"

ANONYMOUS

Brahma

If the red slayer think he slays,
    Or if the slain think he is slain,
They know not well the subtle ways
    I keep, and pass, and turn again.

Far or forgot to me is near;
    Shadow and sunlight are the same;
The vanished gods to me appear;
    And one to me are shame and fame.

They reckon ill who leave me out;
    When me they fly, I am the wings;
I am the doubter and the doubt,
    And I the hymn the Brahmin sings.

The strong gods pine for my abode,
    And pine in vain the sacred Seven;
But thou, meek lover of the good!
    Find me, and turn thy back on heaven.

RALPH WALDO EMERSON

What Was His Creed?

What was his creed?
I do not know his creed, I only know
That here below, he walked the common road
And lifted many a load, lightened the task,
Brightened the day for others toiling on a weary way:
This, his only meed; I do not know his creed.

His creed? I care not what his creed;
Enough that never yielded he to greed,
But served a brother in his daily need;
Plucked many a thorn and planted many a flower;
Glorified the service of each hour;
Had faith in God, himself, and fellow-men;—
Perchance he never thought in terms of creed,
I only know he lived a life, in deed!

H. N. FIFER

Invictus

Out of the night that covers me,
    Black as the Pit from pole to pole,
I thank whatever gods may be
    For my unconquerable soul.

In the fell clutch of circumstance
    I have not winced nor cried aloud.
Under the bludgeonings of chance
    My head is bloody, but unbowed.

Beyond this place of wrath and tears
    Looms but the horror of the shade,
And yet the menace of the years
    Finds, and shall find me, unafraid.

It matters not how strait the gate,
    How charged with punishments the scroll,
I am the master of my fate:
    I am the captain of my soul.

WILLIAM ERNEST HENLEY

Watch Yourself Go By

Just stand aside and watch yourself go by;
Think of yourself as "he" instead of "I."
Note closely as in other men you note
The bag-kneed trousers and the seedy coat.
Pick flaws; find fault; forget the man is you,
And strive to make your estimate ring true.
Confront yourself and look you in the eye—
Just stand aside and watch yourself go by.

Interpret all your motives just as though
You looked on one whose aims you did not know.
Let undisguised contempt surge through you when
You see you shirk, O commonest of men!
Despise your cowardice; condemn whate'er
You note of falseness in you anywhere.
Defend not one defect that shares your eye—
Just stand aside and watch yourself go by.

And then, with eyes unveiled to what you loathe,
To sins that with sweet charity you'd clothe,
Back to your self-walled tenement you'll go
With tolerance for all who dwell below.
The faults of others then will dwarf and shrink,
Love's chain grows stronger by one mighty link,
When you, with "he" as substitute for "I,"
Have stood aside and watched yourself go by.

STRICKLAND GILLILAN

The Character of a Happy Life

How happy is he born and taught
   That serveth not another's will;
Whose armour is his honest thought,
   And simple truth his utmost skill;

Whose passions not his masters are;
   Whose soul is still prepared for death,
Untied unto the world by care
   Of public fame or private breath;

Who envies none that chance doth raise,
   Nor vice; who never understood
How deepest wounds are given by praise;
   Nor rules of state, but rules of good;

Who hath his life from rumours freed;
   Whose conscience is his strong retreat;
Whose state can neither flatterers feed,
   Nor ruin make oppressors great;

Who God doth late and early pray
   More of his grace than gifts to lend;
And entertains the harmless day
   With a religious book or friend.

This man is free from servile bands
   Of hope to rise or fear to fall:
Lord of himself, though not of lands,
   And, having nothing, yet hath all.

SIR HENRY WOOTTON

A Vow for New Year's

Every hour and every minute
Has a New Year's Day tucked in it
And each single one of these
Is packed with possibilities—
Possibilities of pleasure,
Of sharing with some friend some treasure,
Of making a "Good morning" cheery—
Making a good one from a dreary—
Of shutting tight the lips to hide
A bit of gossip safe inside
Instead of letting it get out
To roam about and maybe do
More harm than you would like it to.
Let us take a little vow,
Since it is the New Year now,
To be more kind, more brave, more gay
This year and make each single day
That comes a model New Year's Day!

MARY CAROLYN DAVIES

Success

If you want a thing bad enough
To go out and fight for it,
Work day and night for it,
Give up your time and your peace and your sleep for it
If only desire of it
Makes you quite mad enough
Never to tire of it,
Makes you hold all other things tawdry and cheap for it
If life seems all empty and useless without it
And all that you scheme and you dream is about it,
If gladly you'll sweat for it,
Fret for it,
Plan for it,
Lose all your terror of God or man for it,
If you'll simply go after that thing that you want,
With all your capacity,
Strength and sagacity,
Faith, hope and confidence, stern pertinacity,
If neither cold poverty, famished and gaunt,
Nor sickness nor pain
Of body or brain
Can turn you away from the thing that you want,
If dogged and grim you besiege and beset it,
  You'll get it!

BERTON BRALEY

Faith

An Irish Wish

May the road rise to meet you.
May the wind be ever at your back.
May the Good Lord keep you in the hollow of His hand.
May your heart be as warm as your hearthstone.
And when you come to die may the wail
    of the poor be the only sorrow you'll leave behind.
May God bless you always.

ANONYMOUS

In Sorrow

Gently, Lord, oh, gently lead us,
    Pilgrims in this vale of tears,
Through the trials yet decreed us,
    Till our last great change appears.
When temptation's darts assail us,
    When in devious paths we stray,
Let Thy goodness never fail us,
    Lead us in Thy perfect way.

In the hour of pain and anguish,
    In the hour when death draws near,
Suffer not our hearts to languish,
    Suffer not our souls to fear;
And, when mortal life is ended,
    Bid us in Thine arms to rest,
Till, by angel bands attended,
    We awake among the blest.

THOMAS HASTINGS

A Prayer Found in Chester Cathedral

Give me a good digestion, Lord
    And also something to digest;
Give me a healthy body, Lord,
    With sense to keep it at its best.

Give me a healthy mind, good Lord,
    To keep the good and pure in sight;
Which, seeing sin, is not appalled,
    But finds a way to set it right.

Give me a mind that is not bored,
    That does not whimper, whine or sigh;
Don't let me worry overmuch
    About the fussy thing called "I."

Give me a sense of humor, Lord,
    Give me the grace to see a joke;
To get some happiness from life,
    And pass it on to other folk.

ANONYMOUS

Morning Prayer

When little things would irk me, and I grow
Impatient with my dear one, make me know
How in a moment joy can take its flight
And happiness be quenched in endless night.
Keep this thought with me all the livelong day
That I may guard the harsh words I might say
When I would fret and grumble, fiery hot,
At trifles that tomorrow are forgot—
Let me remember, Lord, how it would be
If these, my loved ones, were not here with me.

ELLA WHEELER WILCOX

My Evening Prayer

If I have wounded any soul to-day,
If I have caused one foot to go astray,
If I have walked in my own wilful way—
   Good Lord, forgive!

If I have uttered idle words or vain,
If I have turned aside from want or pain,
Lest I myself should suffer through the strain—
   Good Lord, forgive!

If I have craved for joys that are not mine,
If I have let my wayward heart repine,
Dwelling on things of earth, not things divine—
   Good Lord, forgive!

If I have been perverse, or hard, or cold,
If I have longed for shelter in Thy fold,
When Thou hast given me some part to hold—
   Good Lord, forgive.

Forgive the sins I have confessed to Thee,
Forgive the secret sins I do not see,
That which I know not, Father, teach Thou me—
   Help me to live.

CHARLES H. GABRIEL

It Might Have Been Worse

Sometimes I pause and sadly think
    Of the things that might have been,
Of the golden chances I let slip by,
    And which never returned again.

Think of the joys that might have been mine;
    The prizes I almost won,
The goals I missed by a mere hair's breadth;
    And the things I might have done.

It fills me with gloom when I ponder thus,
    Till I look on the other side,
How I might have been completely engulfed
    By misfortune's surging tide.

The unknown dangers lurking about,
    Which I passed safely through
The evils and sorrows that I've been spared
    Pass plainly now in review.

So when I am downcast and feeling sad,
    I repeat over and over again,
Things are far from being as bad
    As they easily might have been.

G.J. RUSSELL

Prayer

God, though this life is but a wraith,
    Although we know not what we use,
Although we grope with little faith,
    Give me the heart to fight—and lose.

Ever insurgent let me be,
    Make me more daring than devout;
From sleek contentment keep me free,
    And fill me with a buoyant doubt.

Open my eyes to visions girt
    With beauty, and with wonder lit—
But let me always see the dirt,
    And all that spawn and die in it.

Open my ears to music; let
    Me thrill with Spring's first flutes and drums—
But never let me dare forget
    The bitter ballads of the slums.

From compromise and things half-done,
    Keep me, with stern and stubborn pride.
And when, at last, the fight is won,
    God, keep me still unsatisfied.

LOUIS UNTERMEYER

Say Not the Struggle Naught Availeth

Say not the struggle naught availeth,
　　The labour and the wounds are vain,
The enemy faints not, nor faileth,
　　And as things have been they remain.

If hopes were dupes, fears may be liars;
　　It may be, in yon smoke conceal'd,
Your comrades chase e'en now the fliers,
　　And, but for you, possess the field.

For while the tired waves, vainly breaking,
　　Seem here no painful inch to gain,
Far back, through creeks and inlets making,
　　Comes silent, flooding in, the main.

And not by eastern windows only,
　　When daylight comes, comes in the light;
In front the sun climbs slow, how slowly!
　　But westward, look, the land is bright!

ARTHUR HUGH CLOUGH

Hanukkah Hymn

Rock of Ages, let our song
Praise Thy saving power;
Thou, amidst the raging foes,
Wast our sheltering tower.
Furious, they assailed us,
But Thine arm availed us,
And Thy word
Broke their sword
When our own strength failed us.

Kindling new the holy lamps,
Priest approved in suffering,
Purified the nation's shrine,
Brought to God their offering.
And His courts surrounding,
Hear, in joy abounding,
Happy throngs
Singing songs
With a mighty sounding.

Children of the martyr race,
Whether free or fettered,
Wake the echoes of the songs
Where ye may be scattered.
Yours the message cheering
That the time is nearing
Which will see
All men free,
Tyrants disappearing.

ANONYMOUS

This Prayer I Make

This prayer I make,
Knowing that Nature never did betray
The heart that loved her; 'tis her privilege,
Through all the years of this our life, to lead
From joy to joy: for she can so inform
The mind that is within us, so impress
With quietness and beauty, and so feed
With lofty thoughts, that neither evil tongues,
Rash judgments, nor the sneers of selfish men,
Nor greetings where no kindness is, nor all
The dreary intercourse of daily life,
Shall e'er prevail against us, or disturb
Our cheerful faith, that all which we behold
Is full of blessings.

WILLIAM WORDSWORTH

Prayer of an Unknown Confederate Soldier

I asked God for strength, that I might achieve,
I was made weak, that I might learn humbly to obey . . .
I asked for health, that I might do greater things,
I was given infirmity, that I might do better things . . .
I asked for riches, that I might be happy,
I was given poverty that I might be wise . . .
I asked for power, that I might have the praise of men,
I was given weakness, that I might feel the need of God . . .
I asked for all things, that I might enjoy life,
I was given life, that I might enjoy all things . . .
I got nothing that I asked for—
    but everything that I had hoped for.
Almost despite myself, my unspoiled prayers were answered.
I am among all men, most richly blessed.

My Good Consists in Cleaving to God

(MIHI ADHAERERE DEO BONUM EST)

God be in my hede
And in my understandyng.
God be in myne eyes
And in my lokyng.
God be in my mouth
And in my speakyng.
God be in my harte
And in my thynkyng.
God be at mine ende
And at my departyng.

ANONYMOUS

Light Shining Out of Darkness

God moves in a mysterious way,
    His wonders to perform;
He plants His footsteps in the sea,
    And rides upon the storm.

Deep in unfathomable mines
    Of never-failing skill
He treasures up His bright designs,
    And works His sovereign will.

Ye fearful saints, fresh courage take;
    The clouds ye so much dread
Are big with mercy, and shall break
    In blessings on your head.

Judge not the Lord by feeble sense,
    But trust Him for His grace;
Behind a frowning Providence
    He hides a smiling face.

His purposes will ripen fast,
    Unfolding every hour;
The bud may have a bitter taste,
    But sweet will be the flower.

Blind unbelief is sure to err,
    And scan His work in vain;
God is His own interpreter,
    And He will make it plain.

WILLIAM COWPER

For Those Who Fail

"All honor to him, who shall win the fight,"
The world has cried for a thousand years,
But to him who tries and who fails and dies,
I give great honor and glory and tears;
Give glory and honor and pitiful tears
To all who fail in their deeds sublime;
Their ghosts are many in the van of years,
They were born with time in advance of time.
Oh! great is the hero who wins a name,
But greater many and many a time
Some pale-faced fellow who dies in shame
And lets God publish the thought sublime,
And great is the man with the sword undrawn,
And good is the man who refrains from wine,
But the man who fails and yet still fights on,
Lo, he is a twin brother of mine.

JOAQUIN MILLER

Rock of Ages

Rock of Ages, cleft for me,
Let me hide myself in Thee!
Let the water and the blood,
From Thy riven side which flowed,
Be of sin the double cure—
Cleanse me from its guilt and power.

Not the labors of my hands
Can fulfil Thy law's demands;
Could my zeal no respite know,
Could my tears for ever flow,
All for sin could not atone—
Thou must save, and Thou alone.

Nothing in my hand I bring—
Simply to Thy Cross I cling;
Naked come to Thee for dress—
Helpless look to Thee for grace;
Foul, I to the Fountain fly—
Wash me, Saviour, or I die!

While I draw this fleeting breath,
When my eye-strings break in death,
When I soar to worlds unknown,
See Thee on Thy judgment-throne,
Rock of Ages, cleft for me,
Let me hide myself in Thee!

AUGUSTUS MONTAGUE TOPLADY

Ring Out, Wild Bells

Ring out, wild bells, to the wild sky,
    The flying cloud, the frosty light:
    The year is dying in the night;
Ring out, wild bells, and let him die.

Ring out the old, ring in the new,
    Ring, happy bells, across the snow:
    The year is going, let him go;
Ring out the false, ring in the true.

ALFRED, LORD TENNYSON

"A Mighty Fortress Is Our God"

A mighty fortress is our God,
    A bulwark never failing;
Our helper He amid the flood
    Of mortal ills prevailing.
        For still our ancient foe
        Doth seek to work us woe;
        His craft and power are great,
        And, armed with cruel hate,
On earth is not his equal.

Did we in our own strength confide,
    Our striving would be losing,—
Were not the right man on our side,
    The man of God's own choosing.
        Dost ask who that may be?
        Christ Jesus, it is He,
        Lord Sabaoth His name,
        From age to age the same,
And He must win the battle.

And though this world, with devils filled,
    Should threaten to undo us,
We will not fear, for God hath willed
    His truth to triumph through us.
        The Prince of Darkness grim,—
        We tremble not for him;
        His rage we can endure,
        For lo! his doom is sure:
One little word shall fell him.

That word above all earthly powers,
  No thanks to them, abideth;
The spirit and the gifts are ours
  Through Him who with us sideth.
    Let goods and kindred go,
    This mortal life also;
    The body they may kill,
    God's truth abideth still,
  His Kingdom is forever.

**FROM THE GERMAN OF MARTIN LUTHER,
BY FREDERICK HENRY HEDGE**

Pied Beauty

Glory be to God for dappled things—
    For skies of couple-colour as a brinded cow;
   For rose-moles all in stipple upon trout that swim;
Fresh-firecoal chestnut-falls; finches' wings;
  Landscape plotted and pieced—fold, fallow,
     and plough;
  And all trades, their gear and tackle and trim.

All things counter, original, spare, strange;
  Whatever is fickle, freckled (who knows how?)
   With swift, slow; sweet, sour; adazzle, dim;
He fathers-forth whose beauty is past change:
    Praise him.

GERARD MANLEY HOPKINS

There Is No Death

There is no death! The stars go down
   To rise upon some other shore,
And bright in heaven's jeweled crown
   They shine for evermore.

There is no death! The dust we tread
   Shall change beneath the summer showers
To golden grain or mellow fruit
   Or rainbow-tinted flowers.

There is no death! The leaves may fall,
   The flowers may fade and pass away—
They only wait, through wintry hours,
   The coming of the May.

The bird-like voice, whose joyous tones
   Made glad this scene of sin and strife,
Sings now an everlasting song
   Amid the tree of life.

And ever near us, though unseen,
   The dear immortal spirits tread;
For all the boundless universe
   Is Life—there are no dead!

JOHN LUCKEY MCCREERY

You Mustn't Quit

When things go wrong, as they sometimes will,
When the road you're trudging seems all uphill,
When the funds are low and the debts are high
And you want to smile, but you have to sigh,
When care is pressing you down a bit,
Rest! if you must—but never quit.

Life is queer, with its twists and turns,
As every one of us sometimes learns,
And many a failure turns about
When he might have won if he'd stuck it out;
Stick to your task, though the pace seems slow—
You may succeed with one more blow.

Success is failure turned inside out—
The silver tint of the clouds of doubt—
And you never can tell how close you are,
It may be near when it seems afar;
So stick to the fight when you're hardest hit—
It's when things seem worst that *You Mustn't Quit*.

AUTHOR UNKNOWN

Let Us Have Peace

The earth is weary of our foolish wars.
Her hills and shores were shaped for lovely things,
Yet all our years are spent in bickerings
  Beneath the astonished stars.

April by April laden with beauty comes,
Autumn by Autumn turns our toil to gain,
But hand at sword hilt, still we start and strain
  To catch the beat of drums.

Knowledge to knowledge adding, skill to skill,
We strive for others' good as for our own—
And then, like cavemen snarling with a bone,
  We turn and rend and kill. . . .

With life so fair, and all too short a lease
Upon our special star! Nay, love and trust,
Not blood and thunder shall redeem our dust.
  Let us have peace!

NANCY BYRD TURNER

I Have Found Such Joy

I have found such joy in simple things;
  A plain, clean room, a nut-brown loaf of bread,
A cup of milk, a kettle as it sings,
  The shelter of a roof above my head,
And in a leaf-laced square along the floor,
Where yellow sunlight glimmers through a door.

I have found such joy in things that fill
  My quiet days: a curtain's blowing grace,
A potted plant upon my window sill,
  A rose, fresh-cut and placed within a vase;
A table cleared, a lamp beside a chair,
And books I long have loved beside me there.

Oh, I have found such joys I wish I might
  Tell every woman who goes seeking far
For some elusive, feverish delight,
  That very close to home the great joys are:
The elemental things—old as the race,
Yet never, through the ages, commonplace.

GRACE NOLL CROWELL

Recessional

God of our fathers, known of old—
  Lord of our far-flung battle-line—
Beneath whose awful Hand we hold
  Dominion over palm and pine—
Lord God of Hosts, be with us yet,
Lest we forget, lest we forget!

The tumult and the shouting dies—
  The captains and the kings depart—
Still stands Thine ancient sacrifice,
  An humble and a contrite heart.
Lord God of Hosts, be with us yet,
Lest we forget, lest we forget!

Far-call'd our navies melt away—
  On dune and headland sinks the fire—
Lo, all our pomp of yesterday
  Is one with Nineveh and Tyre!
Judge of the Nations, spare us yet,
Lest we forget, lest we forget!

If, drunk with sight of power, we loose
  Wild tongues that have not Thee in awe—
Such boasting as the Gentiles use
  Or lesser breeds without the Law—
Lord God of Hosts, be with us yet,
Lest we forget, lest we forget!

For heathen heart that puts her trust
  In reeking tube and iron shard—

All valiant dust that builds on dust,
    And guarding calls not Thee to guard—
For frantic boast and foolish word,
Thy Mercy on Thy People, Lord!

RUDYARD KIPLING

Nature

Stranger, if thou hast learned a truth which needs
No school of long experience, that the world
Is full of guilt and misery, and hast seen
Enough of all its sorrows, crimes, and cares,
To tire thee of it, enter this wild wood
And view the haunts of Nature. The calm shade
Shall bring a kindred calm, and the sweet breeze
That makes the green leaves dance, shall waft a balm
To thy sick heart. Thou wilt find nothing here
Of all that pained thee in the haunts of men,
And made thee loathe thy life. The primal curse
Fell, it is true, upon the unsinning earth,
But not in vengeance. God hath yoked to guilt
Her pale tormentor, misery. Hence, these shades
Are still the abodes of gladness; the thick roof
Of green and stirring branches is alive
And musical with birds, that sing and sport
In wantonness of spirit; while below
The squirrel, with raised paws and form erect,
Chirps merrily. Throngs of insects in the shade
Try their thin wings and dance in the warm beam
That waked them into life. Even the green trees
Partake the deep contentment; as they bend
To the soft winds, the sun from the blue sky
Looks in and sheds a blessing on the scene.
Scarce less the cleft-born wild-flower seems to enjoy
Existence than the wingèd plunderer
That sucks its sweets. The mossy rocks themselves,
And the old and ponderous trunks of prostrate trees
That lead from knoll to knoll a causey rude

Or bridge the sunken brook, and their dark roots,
With all their earth upon them, twisting high,
Breathe fixed tranquillity. The rivulet
Sends forth glad sounds, and tripping o'er its bed
Of pebbly sands, or leaping down the rocks,
Seems, with continuous laughter, to rejoice
In its own being. Softly tread the marge,
Lest from her midway perch thou scare the wren
That dips her bill in water. The cool wind,
That stirs the stream in play, shall come to thee,
Like one that loves thee nor will let thee pass
Ungreeted, and shall give its light embrace.

WILLIAM CULLEN BRYANT

The Evening Cloud

A cloud lay cradled near the setting sun,
  A gleam of crimson tinged its braided snow;
Long had I watched the glory moving on
  O'er the still radiance of the lake below.
Tranquil its spirit seemed, and floated slow!
  Even in its very motion there was rest;
While every breath of eve that chanced to blow
  Wafted the traveller to the beauteous west.
Emblem, methought, of the departed soul!
  To whose white robe the gleam of bliss is given,
And by the breath of mercy made to roll
  Right onwards to the golden gates of heaven,
Where to the eye of faith it peaceful lies,
And tells to man his glorious destinies.

JOHN WILSON

Who Has Seen the Wind?

Who has seen the wind?
    Neither I nor you:
But when the leaves hang trembling,
    The wind is passing through.

Who has seen the wind?
    Neither you nor I:
But when the trees bow down their heads,
    The wind is passing by.

CHRISTINA ROSSETTI

The Tiger

Tiger! Tiger! burning bright
In the forests of the night,
What immortal hand or eye
Could frame thy fearful symmetry?

In what distant deeps or skies
Burnt the fire of thine eyes?
On what wings dare he aspire?
What the hand dare seize the fire?

And what shoulder, and what art,
Could twist the sinews of thy heart?
And when thy heart began to beat,
What dread hand? and what dread feet?

What the hammer? what the chain?
In what furnace was thy brain?
What the anvil? what dread grasp
Dare its deadly terrors clasp?

When the stars threw down their spears,
And water'd heaven with their tears,
Did he smile his work to see?
Did he who made the Lamb make thee?

Tiger! Tiger! burning bright
In the forests of the night,
What immortal hand or eye,
Dare frame thy fearful symmetry?

WILLIAM BLAKE

Nightingales

Beautiful must be the mountains whence ye come,
And bright in the fruitful valleys the streams, wherefrom
  Ye learn your song:
Where are those starry woods? O might I wander there,
 Among the flowers, which in that heavenly air
  Bloom the year long!

 Nay, barren are those mountains and spent the streams:
 Our song is the voice of desire, that haunts our dreams,
  A throe of the heart,
Whose pining visions dim, forbidden hopes profound,
 No dying cadence nor long sigh can sound,
  For all our art.

 Alone, aloud in the raptured ear of men
 We pour our dark nocturnal secret; and then,
  As night is withdrawn
From these sweet-springing meads and bursting boughs of
  May,
 Dream, while the innumerable choir of day
  Welcome the dawn.

ROBERT BRIDGES

To the Willow-Tree

Thou art to all lost love the best,
    The only true plant found,
Wherewith young men and maids distressed,
    And left of love, are crowned.

When once the lover's rose is dead,
    Or laid aside forlorn:
Then willow-garlands 'bout the head
    Bedewed with tears are worn.

When with neglect, the lovers' bane,
    Poor maids rewarded be
For their love lost, their only gain
    Is but a wreath from thee.

And underneath thy cooling shade,
    When weary of the light,
The love-spent youth and love-sick maid
    Come to weep out the night.

ROBERT HERRICK

Trees

I think that I shall never see
A poem lovely as a tree.

A tree whose hungry mouth is pressed
Against the earth's sweet flowing breast;

A tree that looks at God all day
And lifts her leafy arms to pray;

A tree that may in summer wear
A nest of robins in her hair;

Upon whose bosom snow has lain;
Who intimately lives with rain.

Poems are made by fools like me,
But only God can make a tree.

JOYCE KILMER

The Beech Tree's Petition

O leave this barren spot to me!
Spare, woodman, spare the beechen tree!
Though bush or floweret never grow
My dark unwarming shade below;
Nor summer bud perfume the dew
Of rosy blush, or yellow hue;
Nor fruits of autumn, blossom-born,
My green and glossy leaves adorn;
Nor murmuring tribes from me derive
Th' ambrosial amber of the hive;
Yet leave this barren spot to me:
Spare, woodman, spare the beechen tree!

Thrice twenty summers I have seen
The sky grow bright, the forest green;
And many a wintry wind have stood
In bloomless, fruitless solitude,
Since childhood in my pleasant bower
First spent its sweet and sportive hour;
Since youthful lovers in my shade
Their vows of truth and rapture made,
And on my trunk's surviving frame
Carved many a long-forgotten name.
Oh! by the sighs of gentle sound,
First breathed upon this sacred ground;
By all that Love has whispered here,
Or Beauty heard with ravished ear;
As Love's own altar honor me:
Spare, woodman, spare the beechen tree!

THOMAS CAMPBELL

To Meadows

Ye have been fresh and green,
    Ye have been fill'd with flowers:
And ye the walks have been
    Where maids have spent their hours.

You have beheld, how they
    With wicker arks did come
To kiss, and bear away
    The richer cowslips home.

Y'ave heard them sweetly sing,
    And seen them in a round:
Each virgin, like a Spring,
    With honeysuckles crown'd.

But now, we see, none here,
    Whose silv'ry feet did tread,
And with dishevell'd hair,
    Adorn'd this smoother mead.

Like unthrifts, having spent
    Your stock, and needy grown,
Y'are left here to lament
    Your poor estate, alone.

ROBERT HERRICK

Written in March

The Cock is crowing,
The stream is flowing,
The small birds twitter,
The lake doth glitter,
The green field sleeps in the sun;
The oldest and youngest
Are at work with the strongest;
The cattle are grazing,
Their heads never raising;
There are forty feeding like one!

Like an army defeated
The snow hath retreated,
And now doth fare ill
On the top of the bare hill;
The ploughboy is whooping—anon—anon
There's joy in the mountains;
There's life in the fountains;
Small clouds are sailing,
Blue sky prevailing;
The rain is over and gone!

WILLIAM WORDSWORTH

Home Thoughts, from Abroad

Oh, to be in England
Now that April's there,
And whoever wakes in England
Sees, some morning, unaware,
That the lowest boughs and the brushwood sheaf
Round the elm-tree bole are in tiny leaf,
While the chaffinch sings on the orchard bough
In England—now!

And after April, when May follows
And the white-throat builds, and all the swallows!
Hark, where my blossomed pear-tree in the hedge
Leans to the field and scatters on the clover
Blossoms and dewdrops—at the bent spray's edge—
That's the wise thrush: he sings each song twice over,
Lest you should think he never could recapture
The first fine careless rapture!
And though the fields look rough with hoary dew,
All will be gay when noontide wakes anew
The buttercups, the little children's dower
—Far brighter than this gaudy melon-flower!

ROBERT BROWNING

The Snow-Storm

Announced by all the trumpets of the sky,
Arrives the snow, and, driving o'er the fields,
Seems nowhere to alight: the whited air
Hides hills and woods, the river, and the heaven,
And veils the farm-house at the garden's end.
The sled and traveller stopped, the courier's feet
Delayed, all friends shut out, the housemates sit
Around the radiant fireplace, enclosed
In a tumultuous privacy of storm.

Come see the north wind's masonry.
Out of an unseen quarry evermore
Furnished with tile, the fierce artificer
Curves his white bastions with projected roof
Round every windward stake, or tree, or door.
Speeding, the myriad-handed, his wild work
So fanciful, so savage, nought cares he
For number or proportion. Mockingly,
On coop or kennel he hangs Parian wreaths;
A swan-like form invests the hidden thorn;
Fills up the farmer's lane from wall to wall,
Maugre the farmer's sighs; and, at the gate,
A tapering turret overtops the work.
And when his hours are numbered, and the world
Is all his own, retiring, as he were not,
Leaves, when the sun appears, astonished Art
To mimic in slow structures, stone by stone,
Built in an age, the mad wind's night-work,
The frolic architecture of the snow.

RALPH WALDO EMERSON

Sonnet on the Sea

It keeps eternal whispering around
  Desolate shores, and with its mighty swell
  Gluts twice ten thousand caverns, till the spell
Of Hecate leaves them their old shadowy sound.
Often 'tis in such gentle temper found,
  That scarcely will the very smallest shell
  Be moved for days from whence it sometime fell,
When last the winds of heaven were unbound.
Oh ye! who have your eye-balls vexed and tired,
  Feast them upon the wideness of the Sea;
Oh ye! whose ears are dinned with uproar rude,
  Or fed too much with cloying melody,—
Sit ye near some old cavern's mouth, and brood
Until ye start, as if the sea-nymphs quired!

JOHN KEATS

On the Grasshopper and Cricket

The poetry of earth is never dead:
  When all the birds are faint with the hot sun.
  And hide in cooling trees, a voice will run
From hedge to hedge about the new-mown mead;
That is the grasshopper's—he takes the lead
  In summer luxury,—he has never done
  With his delights, for when tired out with fun
He rests at ease beneath some pleasant weed.
The poetry of earth is ceasing never:
  On a lone winter evening, when the frost
Has wrought a silence, from the stove there shrills
The cricket's song, in warmth increasing ever,
  And seems to one, in drowsiness half-lost,
The grasshopper's among some grassy hills.

JOHN KEATS

A Glee for Winter

Hence, rude Winter! crabbed old fellow,
Never merry, never mellow!
Well-a-day! in rain and snow
What will keep one's heart aglow?
Groups of kinsmen, old and young,
Oldest they old friends among;
Groups of friends, so old and true
That they seem our kinsmen too;
These all merry all together
Charm away chill Winter weather.

What will kill this dull old fellow?
Ale that's bright, and wine that's mellow!
Dear old songs for ever new;
Some true love, and laughter too;
Pleasant wit, and harmless fun,
And a dance when day is done.
Music, friends so true and tried,
Whispered love by warm fireside,
Mirth at all times all together,
Make sweet May of Winter weather.

ALFRED DOMETT

The Vagabond

(TO AN AIR OF SCHUBERT)

Give to me the life I love,
    Let the lave go by me,
Give the jolly heaven above
    And the byway nigh me.
Bed in the bush with stars to see,
    Bread I dip in the river—
There's the life for a man like me,
    There's the life for ever.

Let the blow fall soon or late,
    Let what will be o'er me;
Give the face of earth around
    And the road before me.
Wealth I seek not, hope nor love,
    Nor a friend to know me;
All I seek, the heaven above
    And the road below me.

Or let autumn fall on me
    Where afield I linger,
Silencing the bird on tree,
    Biting the blue finger.
White as meal the frosty field—
    Warm the fireside haven—
Not to autumn will I yield,
    Not to winter even!

Let the blow fall soon or late,
    Let what will be o'er me;
Give the face of earth around,
    And the road before me.
Wealth I ask not, hope nor love,
    Nor a friend to know me;
All I ask, the heaven above
    And the road below me.

ROBERT LOUIS STEVENSON

"I Wandered Lonely as a Cloud"

I wandered lonely as a cloud
That floats on high o'er vales and hills,
When all at once I saw a crowd,
A host, of golden daffodils;
Beside the lake, beneath the trees,
Fluttering and dancing in the breeze.

Continuous as the stars that shine
And twinkle in the milky way,
They stretched in never-ending line
Along the margin of a bay:
Ten thousand saw I at a glance,
Tossing their heads in sprightly dance.

The waves beside them danced; but they
Out-did the sparkling waves in glee:
A poet could not but be gay,
In such a jocund company:
I gazed—and gazed—but little thought
What wealth the show to me had brought:

For oft, when on my couch I lie
In vacant or in pensive mood,
They flash upon that inward eye
Which is the bliss of solitude;
And then my heart with pleasure fills,
And dances with the daffodils.

WILLIAM WORDSWORTH

Apparently with No Surprise

Apparently with no surprise
To any happy Flower
The Frost beheads it at its play—
In accidental power—
The blonde Assassin passes on—
The Sun proceeds unmoved
To measure off another Day
For an Approving God.

EMILY DICKINSON

"My Heart's in the Highlands"

My heart's in the Highlands, my heart is not here;
My heart's in the Highlands a-chasing the deer;
A-chasing the wild deer, and following the roe,—
My heart's in the Highlands wherever I go.

Farewell to the Highlands, farewell to the North,
The birthplace of valor, the country of worth;
Wherever I wander, wherever I rove,
The hills of the Highlands for ever I love.

Farewell to the mountains high covered with snow;
Farewell to the straths and green valleys below;
Farewell to the forests and wild-hanging woods;
Farewell to the torrents and loud-pouring floods.

My heart's in the Highlands, my heart is not here;
My heart's in the Highlands a-chasing the deer,
A-chasing the wild deer, and following the roe,—
My heart's in the Highlands wherever I go.

ROBERT BURNS

"To One Who Has Been Long in City Pent"

To one who has been long in city pent,
'Tis very sweet to look into the fair
And open face of heaven,—to breathe a prayer
Full in the smile of the blue firmament.
Who is more happy, when, with heart's content,
Fatigued he sinks into some pleasant lair
Of wavy grass, and reads a debonair
And gentle tale of love and languishment?
Returning home at evening, with an ear
Catching the notes of Philomel,—and eye
Watching the sailing cloudlet's bright career,
He mourns that day so soon has glided by,
E'en like the passage of an angel's tear
That falls through the clear ether silently.

JOHN KEATS

When the Frost Is on the Punkin

When the frost is on the punkin and the fodder's in the shock,
And you hear the kyouck and gobble of the struttin' turkey-cock,
And the clackin' of the guineys, and the cluckin' of the hens,
And the rooster's hallylooer as he tiptoes on the fence;
Oh, it's then's the times a feller is a-feelin' at his best,
With the risin' sun to greet him from a night of peaceful rest,
As he leaves the house, bareheaded, and goes out to feed the stock,
When the frost is on the punkin and the fodder's in the shock.

They's something kind o'harty-like about the atmusfere
When the heat of summer's over and the coollin' fall is here.—
Of course we miss the flowers, and the blossoms on the trees,
And the mumble of the hummin'-birds and buzzin' of the bees;
But the air's so appetizin', and the landscape through the haze
Of a crisp and sunny morning of the airly autumn days
Is a pictur' that no painter has the colorin' to mock,—

When the frost is on the punkin and the fodder's in the shock.
The husky, rusty russel of the tossels of the corn,
And the raspin' of the tangled leaves, as golden as the morn;
The stubble in the furries—kind o' lonesome-like, but still
A-preachin' sermuns to us of the barns they growed to fill;
The straw-stack in the medder, and the reaper in the shed;
The hosses in theyr stalls below, the clover overhead,—
Oh, it sets my hart a-clickin' like the tickin' of a clock,
When the frost is on the punkin and the fodder's in the shock!

Then your apples all is gethered, and the ones a feller keeps
Is poured around the celler-floor in red and yeller heaps;
And your cider-makin' 's over, and your wimmern-folks is through
With their mince and apple butter, and theyr souse and saussage,
    too!. . .
I don't know how to tell it—but ef sich a thing could be
As the Angels wantin' boardin', and they'd call around on me—
I'd want to 'commodate 'em—all the whole-indurin' flock—
When the frost is on the punkin and the fodder's in the shock!

JAMES WHITCOMB RILEY

The Lamb

Little Lamb, who made thee?
Dost thou know who made thee,
Gave thee life, and bade thee feed
By the stream and o'er the mead;
Gave thee clothing of delight,
Softest clothing, woolly, bright;
Gave thee such a tender voice,
Making all the vales rejoice?
 Little Lamb, who made thee?
 Dost thou know who made thee?
Little Lamb, I'll tell thee,
Little Lamb, I'll tell thee;
He is called by thy name,
For He calls Himself a Lamb.
He is meek, and He is mild;
He became a little child.
I a child, and thou a lamb,
We are called by His name.
 Little Lamb, God bless thee!
 Little Lamb, God bless thee.

WILLIAM BLAKE

Sea-Fever

I must go down to the seas again, to the lonely sea and the
    sky,
And all I ask is a tall ship and a star to steer her by,
And the wheel's kick and the wind's song and the white sail's
    shaking,
And a gray mist on the sea's face and a gray dawn breaking.

I must go down to the seas again, for the call of the running
    tide
Is a wild call and a clear call that may not be denied;
And all I ask is a windy day with the white clouds flying,
And the flung spray and the blown spume, and the sea-gulls
    crying.

I must go down to the seas again to the vagrant gypsy life.
To the gull's way and the whale's way where the wind's like
    a whetted knife;
And all I ask is a merry yarn from a laughing fellow-rover,
And quiet sleep and a sweet dream when the long trick's
    over.

JOHN MASEFIELD

The Garden

How vainly men themselves amaze
To win the palm, the oak, or bays;
And their incessant labours see
Crowned from some single herb or tree,
Whose short and narrow-vergéd shade
Does prudently their toils upbraid;
While all flow'rs and all trees do close
To weave the garlands of repose.

Fair quiet, have I found thee here,
And innocence, thy sister dear!
Mistaken long, I sought you then
In busy companies of men.
Your sacred plants, if here below,
Only among the plants will grow.
Society is all but rude,
To this delicious solitude.

No white nor red was ever seen
So amorous as this lovely green.
Fond lovers, cruel as their flame,
Cut in these trees their mistress' name.
Little, alas, they know or heed
How far these beauties hers exceed!
Fair trees! wheres'e'er your barks I wound,
No name shall but your own be found.

When we have run our passions' heat,
Love hither makes his best retreat.
The gods, that mortal beauty chase,
Still in a tree did end their race.
Apollo hunted Daphne so,
Only that she might laurel grow;
And Pan did after Syrinx speed,
Not as a nymph, but for a reed.

What wond'rous life is this I lead!
Ripe apples drop about my head;
The luscious clusters of the vine
Upon my mouth do crush their wine;
The nectarine and curious peach
Into my hands themselves do reach;
Stumbling on melons as I pass,
Ensnared with flow'rs, I fall on grass.

Meanwhile the mind, from pleasure less,
Withdraws into its happiness;
The mind, that ocean where each kind
Does straight its own resemblance find;
Yet it creates, transcending these,
Far other worlds and other seas;
Annihilating all that's made
To a green thought in a green shade.

Here at the fountain's sliding foot
Or at some fruit-tree's mossy root,
Casting the body's vest aside,
My soul into the boughs does glide;
There like a bird it sits and sings,
Then whets and combs its silver wings;
And, till prepared for longer flight,
Waves in its plumes the various light.

Such was that happy garden-state,
While Man there walked without a mate.
After a place so pure and sweet,
What other help could yet be meet!
But 'twas beyond a mortal's share
To wander solitary there;
Two paradises 'twere in one
To live in Paradise alone.

How well the skilful gardener drew
Of flow'rs and herbs this dial new,
Where from above the milder sun
Does through a fragrant zodiac run;
And as it works th' industrious bee
Computes its time as well as we.
How could such sweet and wholesome hours
Be reckoned but with herbs and flowers!

ANDREW MARVELL

Heartache

She Dwelt Among the Untrodden Ways

She dwelt among the untrodden ways
   Beside the springs of Dove,
A maid whom there were none to praise
   And very few to love:

A violet by a mossy stone
   Half hidden from the eye.
—Fair as a star, when only one
   Is shining in the sky.

She lived unknown, and few could know
   When Lucy ceased to be;
But she is in her grave, and, oh,
   The difference to me!

WILLIAM WORDSWORTH

He Is Not Dead

I cannot say, and I will not say
That he is dead. He is just away.
With a cheery smile, and a wave of the hand,
He has wandered into an unknown land
And left us dreaming how very fair
It needs must be, since he lingers there.
And you—oh, you, who the wildest yearn
For an old-time step, and the glad return,
Think of him faring on, as dear
In the love of There as the love of Here.
Think of him still as the same. I say,
He is not dead—he is just away.

JAMES WHITCOMB RILEY

I Have a Rendezvous with Death

I have a rendezvous with Death
  At some disputed barricade,
    When Spring comes back with rustling shade
      And apple blossoms fill the air—
I have a rendezvous with Death
  When Spring brings back blue days and fair.

It may be he shall take my hand,
And lead me into his dark land,
  And close my eyes and quench my breath—
It may be I shall pass him still.
  I have a rendezvous with Death
On some scarred slope of battered hill,
  When Spring comes round again this year
  And the first meadow flowers appear.

God knows 'twere better to be deep
Pillowed in silk and scented down,
Where Love throbs out in blissful sleep,
Pulse nigh to pulse, and breath to breath,
Where hushed awakenings are dear . . .

But I've a rendezvous with Death
At midnight in some flaming town,
When Spring trips north again this year;
And I to my pledged word am true,
I shall not fail that rendezvous.

ALAN SEEGER

The Three Fishers

Three fishers went sailing out into the west,—
    Out into the west as the sun went down;
Each thought of the woman who loved him the best,
    And the children stood watching them out of the town;
For men must work, and women must weep,
And there's little to earn, and many to keep,
    Though the harbor bar be moaning.

Three wives sat up in the light-house tower,
    And trimmed the lamps as the sun went down;
And they looked at the squall, and they looked at the
       shower,
    And the rack it came rolling up, ragged and brown;
But men must work, and women must weep,
Though storms be sudden, and waters deep,
    And the harbor bar be moaning.

Three corpses lay out on the shining sands
    In the morning gleam as the tide went down,
And the women are watching and wringing their hands,
    For those who will never come back to the town;
For men must work, and women must weep,—
And the sooner it's over, the sooner to sleep,—
    And good-by to the bar and its moaning.

CHARLES KINGSLEY

Requiescat

Tread lightly, she is near
   Under the snow,
Speak gently, she can hear
   The daisies grow.

All her bright golden hair
   Tarnished with rust,
She that was young and fair
   Fallen to dust.

Lily-like, white as snow,
   She hardly knew
She was a woman, so
   Sweetly she grew.

Coffin-board, heavy stone,
   Lie on her breast;
I vex my heart alone,
   She is at rest.

Peace, peace; she cannot hear
   Lyre or sonnet;
All my life's buried here.
   Heap earth upon it.

OSCAR WILDE

Glee—The Ghosts

In life three ghostly friars were we,
And now three friarly ghosts we be.
Around our shadowy table placed,
The spectral bowl before us floats;
With wine that none but ghosts can taste,
We wash our unsubstantial throats.
Three merry ghosts—three merry ghosts—
   three merry ghosts are we:
Let the ocean be Port, and we'll think it good sport
To be laid in that Red Sea.

With songs that jovial spectres chaunt,
Our old refectory still we haunt.
The traveller hears our midnight mirth:
"O list!" he cries, "the haunted choir!
The merriest ghost that walks the earth,
Is sure the ghost of a ghostly friar."
Three merry ghosts—three merry ghosts—
   three merry ghosts are we:
Let the ocean be Port, and we'll think it good sport
To be laid in that Red Sea.

THOMAS LOVE PEACOCK

My Life Closed Twice

My life closed twice before its close—
It yet remains to see
If Immortality unveil
A third event to me

So huge, so hopeless to conceive
As these that twice befell.
Parting is all we know of heaven,
And all we need of hell.

EMILY DICKINSON

I Shall Not Care

When I am dead and over me bright April
  Shakes out her rain-drenched hair,
Though you should lean above me broken-hearted,
  I shall not care.

I shall have peace, as leafy trees are peaceful
  When rain bends down the bough;
And I shall be more silent and cold-hearted
  Than you are now.

SARA TEASDALE

Miss You

I miss you in the morning, dear,
    When all the world is new;
I know the day can bring no joy
    Because it brings not you.
I miss the well-loved voice of you,
    Your tender smile for me,
The charm of you, the joy of your
    Unfailing sympathy.

The world is full of folks, it's true,
    But there was only one of you.

I miss you at the noontide, dear;
    The crowded city street
Seems but a desert now, I walk
    In solitude complete.
I miss your hand beside my own
    The light touch of your hand,
The quick gleam in the eyes of you
    So sure to understand.

The world is full of folks, it's true,
    But there was only one of you.

I miss you in the evening, dear,
    When daylight fades away;
I miss the sheltering arms of you
    To rest me from the day,
I try to think I see you yet
    There where the firelight gleams—

Weary at last, I sleep, and still
    I miss you in my dreams.

The world is full of folks, it's true,
    But there was only one of you.

ANONYMOUS

Remember

Remember me when I am gone away,
Gone far away into the silent land;
When you can no more hold me by the hand,
Nor I half turn to go, yet turning stay.
Remember me when no more, day by day,
You tell me of our future that you planned;
Only remember me; you understand
It will be late to counsel then or pray.

Yet if you should forget me for a while
And afterwards remember, do not grieve;
For if the darkness and corruption leave
A vestige of the thoughts that once I had,
Better by far you should forget and smile
Than that you should remember and be sad.

CHRISTINA ROSETTI

Annabel Lee

It was many and many a year ago,
  In a kingdom by the sea,
That a maiden there lived whom you may know
  By the name of Annabel Lee;—
And this maiden she lived with no other thought
  Than to love and be loved by me.

She was a child and I was a child,
  In this kingdom by the sea,
But we loved with a love that was more than love—
  I and my Annabel Lee—
With a love that the winged seraphs of Heaven
  Coveted her and me.

And this was the reason that, long ago,
  In this kingdom by the sea,
A wind blew out of a cloud, by night
  Chilling my Annabel Lee;
So that her highborn kinsmen came
  And bore her away from me,
To shut her up in a sepulchre
  In this kingdom by the sea.

The angels, not half so happy in Heaven,
  Went envying her and me:
Yes! that was the reason (as all men know,
  In this kingdom by the sea)
That the wind came out of the cloud, chilling
  And killing my Annabel Lee.

But our love it was stronger by far than the love
   Of those who were older than we—
   Of many far wiser than we—
And neither the angels in Heaven above
   Nor the demons down under the sea,
Can ever dissever my soul from the soul
   Of the beautiful Annabel Lee:—

For the moon never beams without bringing me dreams
   Of the beautiful Annabel Lee;
And the stars never rise but I see the bright eyes
   Of the beautiful Annabel Lee;
And so, all the night-tide, I lie down by the side
Of my darling, my darling, my life and my bridge,
   In her sepulchre there by the sea—
   In her tomb by the sounding sea.

EDGAR ALLAN POE

The Epitaph

Here rests his head upon the lap of earth
  A youth to Fortune and to Fame unknown.
Fair Science frown'd not on his humble birth
  And Melancholy mark'd him for her own.

Large was his bounty, and his soul sincere;
  Heav'n did a recompense as largely send:
He gave to Mis'ry all he had, a tear,
  He gain'd from Heav'n ('twas all he wish'd) a friend.

No farther seek his merits to disclose,
  Or draw his frailties from their dread abode.
(There they alike in trembling hope repose,)
  The bosom of his Father and his God.

THOMAS GRAY

The House on the Hill

They are all gone away,
   The House is shut and still,
There is nothing more to say.

Through broken walls and gray
   The winds blow bleak and shrill;
They are all gone away.

Nor is there one today
   To speak them good or ill:
There is nothing more to say.

Why is it then we stray
   Around that sunken sill?
They are all gone away,

And our poor fancy-play
   For them is wasted skill:
There is nothing more to say.

There is ruin and decay
   In the House on the Hill:
They are all gone away,
There is nothing more to say.

EDWIN ARLINGTON ROBINSON

After Great Pain . . . .

After great pain a formal feeling comes—
The nerves sit ceremonious like tombs;
The stiff Heart questions—was it He that bore?
And yesterday—or centuries before?

The feet mechanical
Go round a wooden way
Of ground or air or Ought, regardless grown,
A quartz contentment like a stone.

This is the hour of lead
Remembered if outlived,
As freezing persons recollect the snow—
First chill, then stupor, then the letting go.

EMILY DICKINSON

Dirge without Music

I am not resigned to the shutting away of loving hearts
    in the hard ground.
So it is, and so it will be, for so it has been,
    time out of mind:
Into the darkness they go, the wise and the lovely.
  Crowned with lilies and with laurel they go;
    but I am not resigned.

Lovers and thinkers, into the earth with you.
Be one with the dull, the indiscriminate dust.
A fragment of what you felt, of what you knew,
A formula, a phrase remains,—but the best is lost.

The answers quick and keen, the honest look,
    the laughter, the love,—
They are gone. They are gone to feed the roses.
  Elegant and curled
Is the blossom. Fragrant is the blossom. I know. But I do
    not approve.
More precious was the light in your eyes than all the
    roses of the world.

Down, down, down into the darkness of the grave
Gently they go, the beautiful, the tender, the kind;
Quietly they go, the intelligent, the witty, the brave.
I know. But I do not approve. And I am not resigned.

EDNA ST. VINCENT MILLAY

Silence

There is a silence where hath been no sound,
There is a silence where no sound may be,
In the cold grave—under the deep, deep sea,
Or in wide desert where no life is found,
Which hath been mute, and still must sleep profound;
No voice is hushed—no life treads silently,
But clouds and cloudy shadows wander free,
That never spoke, over the idle ground:
But in green ruins, in the desolate walls
Of antique palaces, where Man hath been,
Though the dun fox, or wild hyena calls,
And owls, that flit continually between,
Shriek to the echo, and the low winds moan,
There the true Silence is, self-conscious and alone.

THOMAS HOOD

So Live

From "Thanatopsis"

So live that when thy summons comes to join
The innumerable caravan, which moves
To that mysterious realm, where each shall take
His chamber in the silent halls of death,
Thou go not like the quarry slave at night,
Scourged to his dungeon, but, sustained and soothed
By an unfaltering trust, approach thy grave
Like one who wraps the drapery of his couch
About him, and lies down to pleasant dreams.

WILLIAM CULLEN BRYANT

Death, Be Not Proud

Death, be not proud, though some have called thee
　Mighty and dreadful, for thou art not so;
　For those whom thou think'st thou dost overthrow
Die not, poor Death, nor yet canst thou kill me.
From rest and sleep, which but thy pictures be,
　Much pleasure; then from thee much more must flow,
And soonest our best men with thee do go,
Rest of their bones, and soul's delivery.

Thou art slave to fate, chance, kings, and desperate men,
　And dost with poison, war, and sickness dwell;
　And poppy or charms can make us sleep as well
And better than thy stroke; why swell'st thou then?
　One short sleep past, we wake eternally,
　And death shall be no more; Death, thou shalt die.

JOHN DONNE

When I Have Fears

When I have fears that I may cease to be
Before my pen has glean'd my teeming brain,
Before high-piled books, in charact'ry
Hold like rich garners the full-ripen'd grain;

When I behold, upon the night's starr'd face,
Huge cloudy symbols of a high romance,
And think that I may never live to trace
Their shadows, with the magic hand of chance

And when I feel, fair Creature of an hour!
That I shall never look upon thee more,
Never have relish in the faery power
Of unreflecting love—then on the shore

Of the wide world I stand alone, and think
Till Love and Fame to nothingness do sink.

JOHN KEATS

Nature

As a fond mother, when the day is o'er,
  Leads by the hand her little child to bed,
  Half willing, half reluctant to be led,
  And leave his broken playthings on the floor,
Still gazing at them through the open door,
  Nor wholly reassured and comforted
  By promises of others in their stead,
  Which, though more splendid, may not
    please him more;
So Nature deals with us, and takes away
  Our playthings one by one, and by the hand
  Leads us to rest so gently, that we go
Scarce knowing if we wish to go or stay,
  Being too full of sleep to understand
  How far the unknown transcends the what
    we know.

HENRY WADSWORTH LONGFELLOW

Good-bye

Good-bye, proud world! I'm going home:
Thou art not my friend, and I'm not thine.
Long through thy weary crowds I roam;
A river-ark on the ocean brine,
Long I've been tossed like the driven foam;
But now, proud world! I'm going home.

Good-bye to Flattery's fawning face;
To Grandeur with his wise grimace;
To upstart Wealth's averted eye;
To supple Office, low and high;
To crowded halls, to court and street;
To frozen hearts and hasting feet;
To those who go, and those who come;
Good-bye, proud world! I'm going home.

I am going to my own hearth-stone,
Bosomed in yon green hills alone—
A secret nook in a pleasant land,
Whose groves the frolic fairies planned;
Where arches green, the livelong day,
Echo the blackbird's roundelay,
And vulgar feet have never trod
A spot that is sacred to thought and God.

O, when I am safe in my sylvan home,
I tread on the pride of Greece and Rome;
And when I am stretched beneath the pines,
Where the evening star so holy shines,
I laugh at the lore and the pride of man,

At the sophist schools and the learned clan;
For what are they all, in their high conceit,
When man in the bush with God may meet?

RALPH WALDO EMERSON

Mother

Again your kindly, smiling face I see.
Do I but dream? And do my eyes deceive?
Again you whisper through the years to me,
I feel the pressure of your lips at eve.
I dream once more I sit upon your knee,
And hear sweet counsel that I should not grieve;
My hand in yours at twilight time as we
Talk low, and I your sweet caress receive.
At times I see your face with sorrow wrung,
Until, somewhat confused, I scarce believe
That I still dream. Your friends when you were young,
Your own great hopes, your cheer and laughter free
In some weird way are strangely haunting me.
O mother of my childhood's pleasant days!
Still whispering courage and dispelling fears
In daylight hours or quiet moonlight rays,
Are you a dream come from my younger years?
Or do you really walk along the ways,
And know my triumphs, or my inner tears,
That quickly cease when you close by me seem?
Let me sleep on, dear God, if I but dream.

MAX EHRMANN

At the Mid Hour of Night . . .

At the mid hour of night, when stars are weeping, I fly
To the lone vale we loved, when life shone warm in thine eye;
   And I think oft, if spirits can steal from the regions of air
    To revisit past scenes of delight, thou wilt come to me there,
And tell me our love is remembered even in the sky.

Then I sing the wild song it once was rapture to hear,
When our voices commingling breathed like one on the ear;
   And as Echo far off through the vale my sad orison rolls,
    I think, O my love! 'tis thy voice from the Kingdom of Souls
Faintly answering still the notes that once were so dear.

THOMAS MOORE

On My First Son

Farewell, thou child of my right hand, and joy;
  My sin was too much hope of thee, loved boy.
Seven years thou wert lent to me, and I thee pay,
  Exacted by thy fate, on the just day.
Oh, could I lose all father now! For why
  Will man lament the state he should envy?
To have so soon 'scaped world's and flesh's rage,
  And, if no other misery, yet age?
Rest in soft peace, and, asked, say here doth lie
  Ben Jonson his best piece of poetry;
For whose sake, henceforth, all his vows be such,
  As what he loves may never like too much.

BEN JONSON

Elegy Written in a Country Churchyard

The curfew tolls the knell of parting day,
  The lowing herd winds slowly o'er the lea,
The plowman homeward plods his weary way,
  And leaves the world to darkness and to me.

Now fades the glimmering landscape on the sight,
  And all the air a solemn stillness holds,
Save where the beetle wheels his droning flight,
  And drowsy tinklings lull the distant folds;

Save that from yonder ivy-mantled tow'r
  The moping owl does to the moon complain
Of such, as wand'ring near her secret bow'r,
  Molest her ancient solitary reign.

Beneath those rugged elms, that yew-tree's shade,
  Where leaves the turf in many a mould'ring heap,
Each in his narrow cell for ever laid,
  The rude Forefathers of the hamlet sleep.

The breezy call of incense-breathing Morn,
  The swallow twittering from the straw-built shed,
The cock's shrill clarion, or the echoing horn,
  No more shall rouse them from their lowly bed.

For them no more the blazing hearth shall burn,
  Or busy housewife ply her evening care:
No children run to lisp their sire's return,
  Or climb his knees the envied kiss to share.

Oft did the harvest to their sickle yield,
  Their furrow oft the stubborn glebe has broke:
How jocund did they drive their team afield!
  How bow'd the woods beneath their sturdy stroke!

Let not Ambition mock their useful toil,
  Their homely joys, and destiny obscure;
Nor Grandeur hear with a disdainful smile,
  The short and simple annals of the poor.

The boast of heraldry, the pomp of pow'r,
  And all that beauty, all that wealth e'er gave,
Awaits alike th' inevitable hour:
  The paths of glory lead but to the grave.

Nor you, ye proud, impute to these the fault,
  If Memory o'er their tomb no trophies raise.
Where through the long-drawn aisle and fretted vault
  The pealing anthem swells the note of praise.

Can storied urn or animated bust
  Back to its mansion call the fleeting breath?
Can Honour's voice provoke the silent dust,
  Or Flatt'ry soothe the dull cold ear of death?

Perhaps in this neglected spot is laid
  Some heart once pregnant with celestial fire;
Hands that the rod of empire might have sway'd
  Or waked to ecstasy the living lyre.

But Knowledge to their eyes her ample page
  Rich with the spoils of time did ne'er unroll;
Chill Penury repress'd their noble rage,
  And froze the genial current of the soul.

Full many a gem of purest ray serene,
  The dark unfathom'd caves of ocean bear:
Full many a flower is born to blush unseen,
  And waste its sweetness on the desert air.

Some village Hampden that with dauntless breast
  The little tyrant of his fields withstood;
Some mute inglorious Milton here may rest,
  Some Cromwell guiltless of his country's blood.

Th' applause of list'ning senates to command,
  The threats of pain and ruin to despise,
To scatter plenty o'er a smiling land,
  And read their history in a nation's eyes,

Their lot forbade: nor circumscribed alone
  Their growing virtues, but their crimes confined;
Forbade to wade through slaughter to a throne,
  And shut the gates of mercy on mankind.

The struggling pangs of conscious truth to hide,
  To quench the blushes of ingenuous shame,
Or heap the shrine of Luxury and Pride
  With incense kindled at the Muse's flame.

Far from the madding crowd's ignoble strife,
  Their sober wishes never learn'd to stray;
Along the cool sequester'd vale of life
  They kept the noiseless tenor of their way.

Yet ev'n these bones from insult to protect,
  Some frail memorial still erected nigh,
With uncouth rhymes and shapeless sculpture deck
  Implores the passing tribute of a sigh.

Their name, their years, spelt by th' unletter'd Muse,
  The place of fame and elegy supply:
And many a holy text around she strews,
  That teach the rustic moralist to die.

For who, to dumb Forgetfulness a prey,
  This pleasing anxious being e'er resign'd,
Left the warm precincts of the cheerful day,
  Nor cast one longing lingering look behind?

On some fond breast the parting soul relies,
  Some pious drops the closing eye requires;
E'en from the tomb the voice of Nature cries,
  E'en in our ashes live their wonted fires.

For thee, who, mindful of th' unhonour'd dead,
  Dost in these lines their artless tale relate;
If chance, by lonely contemplation led,
  Some kindred spirit shall inquire thy fate.

Haply some hoary-headed swain may say,
  "Oft have we seen him at the peep of dawn
Brushing with hasty steps the dews away
  To meet the sun upon the upland lawn.

"There at the foot of yonder nodding beech
  That wreathes its old fantastic roots so high,
His listless length at noontide would he stretch,
  And pore upon the brook that babbles by.

"Hard by yon wood, now smiling as in scorn,
  Muttering his wayward fancies he would rove;
Now drooping, woeful-wan, like one forlorn,
  Or crazed with care, or cross'd in hopeless love.

"One morn I miss'd him on the custom'd hill,
  Along the heath, and near his fav'rite tree;
Another came, nor yet beside the rill,
  Nor up the lawn, nor at the wood was he;

"The next, with dirges due in sad array
  Slow through the church-way path we saw him borne,
Approach and read (for thou canst read) the lay
  Graved on the stone beneath yon aged thorn."

Aging

The Human Seasons

Four Seasons fill the measure of the year;
There are four seasons in the mind of man:
He has his lusty Spring, when fancy clear
Takes in all beauty with an easy span:

He has his Summer, when luxuriously
Spring's honeyed cud of youthful thought he loves
To ruminate, and by such dreaming high
Is nearest unto Heaven: quiet coves

His soul has in its Autumn, when his wings
He furleth close; contented so to look
On mists in idleness—to let fair things
Pass by unheeded as a threshold brook:—

He has his Winter too of pale misfeature,
Or else he would forego his mortal nature.

JOHN KEATS

Growing Old

The days grow shorter, the nights grow longer;
  The headstones thicken along the way;
And life grows sadder, but love grows stronger
  For those who walk with us day by day.

The tear comes quicker, the laugh comes slower;
  The courage is lesser to do and dare;
And the tide of joy in the heart falls lower,
  And seldom covers the reefs of care.

But all true things in the world seem truer,
  And the better things of earth seem best,
And friends are dearer, as friends are fewer,
  And love is all as our sun dips west

Then let us clasp hands as we walk together,
  And let us speak softly in low, sweet tone,
For no man knows on the morrow whether
  We two pass on—or but one alone.

ELLA WHEELER WILCOX

My Birth-Day

"My birth-day"—what a different sound
　　That word had in my youthful ears!
And how, each time the day comes round,
　　Less and less white its mark appears!
When first our scanty years are told,
It seems like pastime to grow old;
And, as Youth counts the shining links
　　That Time around him binds so fast,
Pleased with the task, he little thinks
　　How hard that chain will press at last.
Vain was the man, and false as vain,
　　Who said—"were he ordained to run
His long career of life again,
　　He would do all that he had done."

Ah, 'tis not thus the voice, that dwells
　　In sober birth-days, speaks to me;
Far otherwise—of time it tells
　　Lavished unwisely, carelessly;
Of counsel mocked: of talents, made
　　Haply for high and pure designs,

But oft, like Israel's incense, laid
　　Upon unholy, earthly shrines;
Of nursing many a wrong desire;
　　Of wandering after Love too far,
And taking every meteor-fire
　　That crossed my pathway, for a star.
All this it tells, and, could I trace
　　The imperfect picture o'er again,

With power to add, retouch, efface
    The lights and shades, the joy and pain,
How little of the past would stay!
How quickly all should melt away—
All—but that Freedom of the Mind,
    Which hath been more than wealth to me;
Those friendships, in my boyhood twined,
    And kept till now unchangingly;
And that dear home, that saving-ark,
    Where Love's true light at last I've found,
Cheering within, when all grows dark,
    And comfortless, and stormy round!

THOMAS MOORE

I Remember, I Remember

I remember, I remember,
  The house where I was born,
The little window where the sun
  Came peeping in at morn:
He never came a wink too soon,
  Nor brought too long a day;
But now, I often wish the night
  Had borne my breath away.

I remember, I remember,
  The roses, red and white;
The violets and the lily-cups,
  Those flowers made of light!
The lilacs where the robin built,
  And where my brother set
The laburnum on his birthday,—
  The tree is living yet!

I remember, I remember,
  Where I was used to swing;
And thought the air must rush as fresh
  To swallows on the wing:
My spirit flew in feathers then,
  That is so heavy now,
And summer pools could hardly cool
  The fever on my brow!

I remember, I remember,
   The fir trees dark and high;
I used to think their slender tops
   Were close against the sky:
It was a childish ignorance,
   But now 'tis little joy
To know I'm farther off from heaven
   Than when I was a boy.

THOMAS HOOD

The Old Familiar Faces

I have had playmates, I have had companions,
In my days of childhood, in my joyful school-days,
All, all are gone, the old familiar faces.

I have been laughing, I have been carousing,
Drinking late, sitting late, with my bosom cronies,
All, all are gone, the old familiar faces.

I loved a love once, fairest among women;
Closed are her doors on me, I must not see her—
All, all are gone, the old familiar faces.

I have a friend, a kinder friend has no man;
Like an ingrate, I left my friend abruptly;
Left him, to muse on the old familiar faces.

Ghost-like I paced round the haunts of my childhood.
Earth seemed a desert I was bound to traverse,
Seeking to find the old familiar faces.

Friend of my bosom, thou more than a brother,
Why wert not thou born in my father's dwelling?
So might we talk of the old familiar faces—

How some they have died, and some they have left me,
And some are taken from me; all are departed;
All, all are gone, the old familiar faces.

CHARLES LAMB

Song

When I am dead, my dearest,
 Sing no sad songs for me;
Plant thou no roses at my head,
 Nor shady cypress tree:
Be the green grass above me
 With showers and dewdrops wet;
And if thou wilt, remember,
 And if thou wilt, forget.

I shall not see the shadows,
 I shall not feel the rain;
I shall not hear the nightingale
 Sing on, as if in pain;
And dreaming through the twilight
 That doth not rise nor set,
Haply I may remember,
 And haply may forget.

CHRISTINA GEORGINA ROSSETTI

'Tis the Last Rose of Summer

'Tis the last rose of summer
   Left blooming alone;
All her lovely companions
   Are faded and gone;
No flower of her kindred,
   No rosebud, is nigh,
To reflect back her blushes,
   To give sigh for sigh.

I'll not leave thee, thou lone one,
   To pine on the stem;
Since the lovely are sleeping,
   Go sleep thou with them.
Thus kindly I scatter
   Thy leaves o'er the bed,
Where thy mates of the garden
   Lie scentless and dead.

So soon may I follow
   When friendships decay,
And from Love's shining circle
   The gems drop away!
When true hearts lie wither'd,
   And fond ones are flown,
Oh! who would inhabit
   This bleak world alone?

THOMAS MOORE

The Oak

Live thy Life,
   Young and old,
Like yon oak,
Bright in spring,
   Living gold;
Summer-rich
   Then; and then
Autumn-changed,
Soberer-hued
   Gold again.

All his leaves
   Fallen at length,
Look, he stands,
Trunk and bough,
   Naked strength.

ALFRED, LORD TENNYSON

My Lost Youth

Often I think of the beautiful town
   That is seated by the sea;
Often in thought go up and down
The pleasant streets of that dear old town,
   And my youth comes back to me.
      And a verse of a Lapland song
      Is haunting my memory still:
      "A boy's will is the wind's will,
And the thoughts of youth are long, long thoughts."

I can see the shadowy lines of its trees,
   And catch, in sudden gleams,
The sheen of the far-surrounding seas,
And islands that were the Hesperides
   Of all my boyish dreams.
      And the burden of that old song,
      It murmurs and whispers still:
      "A boy's will is the wind's will,
And the thoughts of youth are long, long thoughts."

I remember the black wharves and the slips,
   And the sea-tides tossing free;
And Spanish sailors with bearded lips,
And the beauty and mystery of the ships,
   And the magic of the sea.
      And the voice of that wayward song
      Is singing and saying still:
      "A boy's will is the wind's will,
And the thoughts of youth are long, long thoughts."

I remember the bulwarks by the shore,
  And the fort upon the hill;
The sunrise gun, with its hollow roar,
The drum-beat repeated o'er and o'er,
  And the bugle wild and shrill.
    And the music of that old song
    Throbs in my memory still:
    "A boy's will is the wind's will,
And the thoughts of youth are long, long thoughts."

I remember the sea-fight far away,
  How it thundered o'er the tide!
And the dead captains, as they lay
In their graves, o'erlooking the tranquil bay
  Where they in battle died.
    And the sound of that mournful song
    Goes through me with a thrill:
    "A boy's will is the wind's will,
And the thoughts of youth are long, long thoughts."

I can see the breezy dome of groves,
  The shadows of Deering's Woods;
And the friendships old and the early loves
Come back with a Sabbath sound, as of doves
  In quiet neighborhoods.
    And the verse of that sweet old song,
    It flutters and murmurs still:
    "A boy's will is the wind's will,
And the thoughts of youth are long, long thoughts."

I remember the gleams and glooms that dart
  Across the school-boy's brain;
The song and the silence in the heart,
That in part are prophecies, and in part
  Are longings wild and vain.
    And the voice of that fitful song
    Sings on, and is never still:
    "A boy's will is the wind's will,
And the thoughts of youth are long, long thoughts."

There are things of which I may not speak;
  There are dreams that cannot die;
There are thoughts that make the strong heart weak,
And bring a pallor into the cheek,
  And a mist before the eye.
    And the words of that fatal song
    Come over me like a chill:
    "A boy's will is the wind's will,
And the thoughts of youth are long, long thoughts."

Strange to me now are the forms I meet
  When I visit the dear old town;
But the native air is pure and sweet,
And the trees that o'ershadow each well-known street,
  As they balance up and down,
    Are singing the beautiful song,
    Are sighing and whispering still:
    "A boy's will is the wind's will,
And the thoughts of youth are long, long thoughts."

And Deering's Woods are fresh and fair,
   And with joy that is almost pain
My heart goes back to wander there,
And among the dreams of the days that were,
   I find my lost youth again.
      And the strange and beautiful song,
      The groves are repeating it still:
      "A boy's will is the wind's will,
And the thoughts of youth are long, long thoughts."

HENRY WADSWORTH LONGFELLOW

Crossing the Bar

Sunset and evening star,
  And one clear call for me!
And may there be no moaning of the bar,
  When I put out to sea,

But such a tide as moving seems asleep,
  Too full of sound and foam,
When that which drew from out the boundless deep
  Turns again home.

Twilight and evening bell,
  And after that the dark!
And may there be no sadness of farewell,
  When I embark;

For though from out our bourne of Time and Place
  The flood may bear me far,
I hope to see my Pilot face to face
  When I have crost the bar.

ALFRED, LORD TENNYSON

The Old Song

When all the world is young, lad,
   And all the trees are green;
And every goose a swan, lad,
   And every lass a queen;
Then hey for boot and horse, lad,
   And round the world away!
Young blood must have its course, lad,
   And every dog his day.

When all the world is old, lad,
   And all the trees are brown;
And all the sport is stale, lad,
   And all the wheels run down;
Creep home, and take your place there
   The spent and maim'd among;
God grant you find one face there
   You loved when all was young!

CHARLES KINGSLEY

The Old Man's Comforts and How He Gained Them

"You are old, Father William," the young man cried;
  "The few locks which are left you are gray;
You are hale, Father William,—a hearty old man:
  Now tell me the reason, I pray."

"In the days of my youth," Father William replied,
  "I remembered that youth would fly fast,
And abused not my health and my vigor at first,
  That I never might need them at last."

"You are old, Father William," the young man cried,
  "And pleasures with youth pass away;
And yet you lament not the days that are gone:
  Now tell me the reason, I pray."

"In the days of my youth," Father William replied,
  "I remembered that youth could not last;
I thought of the future, whatever I did,
  That I never might grieve for the past."

"You are old, Father William," the young man cried,
  "And life must be hastening away;
You are cheerful, and love to converse upon death:
  Now tell me the reason, I pray."

"I am cheerful, young man," Father William replied;
  "Let the cause thy attention engage;
In the days of my youth, I remembered my God,
  And He hath not forgotten my age."

ROBERT SOUTHEY

Friends Departed

They are all gone into the world of light!
  And I alone sit ling'ring here;
Their very memory is fair and bright,
  And my sad thoughts doth clear.

It glows and glitters in my cloudy breast,
  Like stars upon some gloomy grove,
Or those faint beams in which this hill is drest
  After the sun's remove.

I see them walking in an air of glory,
  Whose light doth trample on my days:
My days, which are at best but dull and hoary,
  Mere glimmering and decays.

O holy Hope! and high Humility,
  High as the heavens above!
These are your walks, and you have show'd them me,
  To kindle my cold love.

Dear, beauteous Death! the jewel of the Just,
  Shining nowhere, but in the dark;
What mysteries do lie beyond thy dust,
  Could man outlook that mark!

He that hath found some fledg'd bird's nest may know,
  At first sight, if the bird be flown;
But what fair well or grove he sings in now,
  That is to him unknown.

And yet as Angels in some brighter dreams
  Call to the soul, when man doth sleep:
So some strange thoughts transcend our wonted themes,
   And into glory peep.

If a star were confin'd into a tomb,
  Her captive flames must needs burn there;
But when the hand that lock'd her up gives room,
   She'll shine through all the sphere.

O Father of eternal life, and all
  Created glories under Thee!
Resume Thy spirit from this world of thrall
   Into true liberty.

Either disperse these mists, which blot and fill
  My perspective still as they pass:
Or else remove me hence unto that hill,
   Where I shall need no glass.

HENRY VAUGHAN

When You Are Old

When you are old and gray and full of sleep,
And nodding by the fire, take down this book,
And slowly read, and dream of the soft look
Your eyes had once, and of their shadows deep;

How many loved your moments of glad grace,
And loved your beauty with love false or true;
But one man loved the pilgrim soul in you,
And loved the sorrows of your changing face.

And bending down beside the glowing bars,
Murmur, a little sadly, how love fled
And paced upon the mountains overhead
And hid his face amid a crowd of stars.

WILLIAM BUTLER YEATS

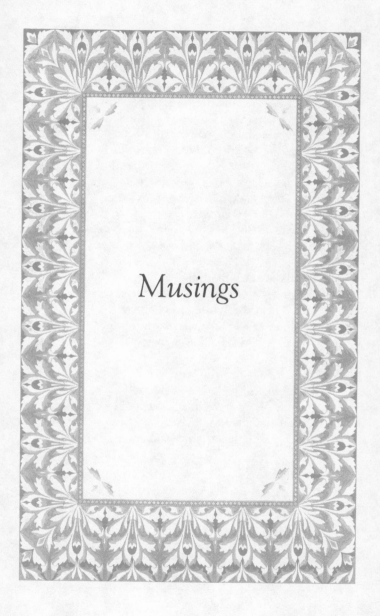

Musings

The Road Not Taken

Two roads diverged in a yellow wood,
And sorry I could not travel both
And be one traveler, long I stood
And looked down one as far as I could
To where it bent in the undergrowth;

Then took the other, as just as fair,
And having perhaps the better claim,
Because it was grassy and wanted wear;
Though as for that the passing there
Had worn them really about the same,

And both that morning equally lay
In leaves no step had trodden black.
Oh, I kept the first for another day!
Yet knowing how way leads on to way,
I doubted if I should ever come back.

I shall be telling this with a sigh
Somewhere ages and ages hence:
Two roads diverged in a wood, and I—
I took the one less traveled by,
And that has made all the difference.

ROBERT FROST

Mother's Hands

Dear gentle hands have stroked my hair
    And cooled my brow,
Soft hands that pressed me close
    And seemed to know somehow
Those fleeting moods and erring thoughts
    That cloud my day,
Which quickly melt beneath their suffrage
    And pass away.

No other balm for earthly pain
    Is half so sure,
No sweet caress so filled with love
    Nor half so pure,
No other soul so close akin that understands,
No touch that brings such perfect peace as Mother's hands.

W. DAYTON WEDGEFARTH

To-Day

So here hath been dawning
    Another blue Day:
Think, wilt thou let it
    Slip useless away?

Out of Eternity
    This new Day is born;
Into Eternity,
    At night, will return.

Behold it aforetime
    No eye ever did:
So soon it for ever
    From all eyes is hid.

Here hath been dawning
    Another blue Day:
Think, wilt thou let it
    Slip useless away?

THOMAS CARLYLE

A Wise Old Owl

A wise old owl lived in an oak;
The more he saw the less he spoke;
The less he spoke the more he heard:
Why can't we all be like that bird?

ANONYMOUS

Who Hath a Book

Who hath a book
   Has friends at hand,
And gold and gear
   At his command;

And rich estates,
   If he but look,
Are held by him
   Who hath a book.

Who hath a book
   Has but to read
And he may be
   A king indeed;

His Kingdom is
   His inglenook;
All this is his
   Who hath a book.

WILBUR D. NESBIT

The Arrow and the Song

I shot an arrow into the air,
It fell to earth, I knew not where;
For, so swiftly it flew, the sight
Could not follow it in its flight.

I breathed a song into the air,
It fell to earth, I knew not where;
For who has sight so keen and strong,
That it can follow the flight of song?

Long, long afterward, in an oak
I found the arrow, still unbroke;
And the song, from beginning to end,
I found again in the heart of a friend.

HENRY WADSWORTH LONGFELLOW

Stanzas

Often rebuked, yet always back returning
　To those first feelings that were born with me,
And leaving busy chase of wealth and learning
　For idle dreams of things that cannot be:

To-day, I will seek not the shadowy region;
　Its unsustaining vastness waxes drear;
And visions rising, legion after legion,
　Bring the unreal world too strangely near.

I'll walk, but not in old heroic traces,
　And not in paths of high morality,
And not among the half-distinguished faces,
　The clouded forms of long-past history.

I'll walk where my own nature would be leading:
　It vexes me to choose another guide:
Where the gray flocks in ferny glens are feeding;
　Where the wild wind blows on the mountain side.

What have those lonely mountains worth revealing?
　More glory and more grief than I can tell:
The earth that wakes *one* human heart to feeling
　Can center both the worlds of Heaven and Hell.

EMILY BRONTË

The Good Great Man

How seldom, friend, a good great man inherits
  Honor and wealth, with all his worth and pains!
It seems a story from the world of spirits
When any man obtains that which he merits,
  Or any merits that which he obtains.

For shame, my friend! renounce this idle strain!
What wouldst thou have a good great man obtain?
Wealth, title, dignity, a golden chain,
Or heap of corpses which his sword hath slain?
Goodness and greatness are not means, but ends.

Hath he not always treasures, always friends,
The great good man? Three treasures,—love, and light,
  And calm thoughts, equable as infant's breath;
And three fast friends, more sure than day or night,—
  Himself, his Maker, and the angel Death.

SAMUEL TAYLOR COLERIDGE

Solitude

Laugh, and the world laughs with you;
    Weep, and you weep alone,
For the sad old earth must borrow its mirth,
    But has trouble enough of its own.
Sing, and the hills will answer;
    Sigh, it is lost on the air,
The echoes bound to a joyful sound,
    But shrink from voicing care.

Rejoice, and men will seek you;
    Grieve, and they turn and go.
They want full measure of all your pleasure,
    But they do not need your woe.
Be glad, and your friends are many;
    Be sad, and you lose them all,—
There are none to decline your nectared wine,
    But alone you must drink life's gall.

Feast, and your halls are crowded;
    Fast, and the world goes by.
Succeed and give, and it helps you live,
    But no man can help you die.
There is room in the halls of pleasure
    For a long and lordly train,
But one by one we must all file on
    Through the narrow aisles of pain.

ELLA WHEELER WILCOX

Farewell, Ungrateful Traitor

Farewell, ungrateful traitor,
   Farewell, my perjured swain;
Let never injured creature
   Believe a man again.
The pleasure of possessing
Surpasses all expressing,
But 'tis too short a blessing,
   And love too long a pain.

'Tis easy to deceive us
   In pity of your pain,
But when we love you leave us
   To rail at you in vain.
Before we have described it,
There is no bliss beside it,
But she that once has tried it,
   Will never love again.
The passion you pretended
   Was only to obtain,
But when the charm is ended
   The charmer you disdain.
Your love by ours we measure
Till we have lost our treasure,
But dying is a pleasure,
   When living is a pain.

JOHN DRYDEN

Richard Cory

Whenever Richard Cory went down town,
  We people on the pavement looked at him;
He was a gentleman from sole to crown,
  Clean favored, and imperially slim.

And he was always quietly arrayed,
  And he was always human when he talked;
But still he fluttered pulses when he said,
  "Good-morning," and he glittered when he walked.

And he was rich—yes, richer than a king—
  And admirably schooled in every grace:
In fine, we thought that he was everything
  To make us wish that we were in his place.

So on we worked, and waited for the light,
  And went without the meat, and cursed the bread;
And Richard Cory, one calm summer night,
  Went home and put a bullet through his head.

EDWIN ARLINGTON ROBINSON

On File

If an unkind word appears,
    File the thing away.
If some novelty in jeers,
    File the thing away.
If some clever little bit
Of a sharp and pointed wit,
Carrying a sting with it—
    File the thing away.

If some bit of gossip come,
    File the thing away.
Scandalously spicy crumb,
    File the thing away.
If suspicion comes to you
That your neighbor isn't true
Let me tell you what to do—
    File the thing away.

Do this for a little while,
Then go out and burn the file.

JOHN KENDRICK BANGS

What Is Good

"What is the real good?"
I asked in musing mood.

Order, said the law court;
Knowledge, said the school;
Truth, said the wise man;
Pleasure, said the fool;
Love, said the maiden;
Beauty, said the page;
Freedom, said the dreamer;
Home, said the sage;
Fame, said the soldier;
Equity, the seer;—

Spake my heart full sadly,
"The answer is not here."

Then within my bosom
Softly this I heard:
"Each heart holds the secret;
Kindness is the word."

JOHN BOYLE O'REILLY

The Lady Poverty

I met her on the Umbrian Hills,
    Her hair unbound, her feet unshod;
As one whom secret glory fills
    She walked—alone with God.

I met her in the city street;
    Oh, how changed was her aspect then!
With heavy eyes and weary feet
    She walked alone—with men.

EVELYN UNDERHILL

My Early Home

Here sparrows build upon the trees,
　　And stockdove hides her nest;
The leaves are winnowed by the breeze
　　Into a calmer rest:
The black-cap's song was very sweet,
　　That used the rose to kiss;
It made the Paradise complete:
　　My early home was this.

The red-breast from the sweetbrier bush
　　Dropped down to pick the worm;
On the horse-chestnut sang the thrush,
　　O'er the house where I was born;
The moonlight, like a shower of pearls,
　　Fell o'er this 'bower of bliss,'
And on the bench sat boys and girls:
　　My early home was this.

The old house stooped just like a cave,
　　Thatched o'er with mosses green;
Winter around the walls would rave,
　　But all was calm within;

The trees are here all green again,
　　Here bees the flowers still kiss,
But flowers and trees seemed sweeter then:
　　My early home was this.

JOHN CLARE

Music, When Soft Voices Die

Music, when soft voices die,
Vibrates in the memory;
Odours, when sweet violets sicken,
Live within the sense they quicken.

Rose leaves, when the rose is dead,
Are heaped for the beloved's bed;
And so thy thoughts, when thou art gone,
Love itself shall slumber on.

PERCY BYSSHE SHELLEY

Song

Stay, stay at home, my heart, and rest;
Home-keeping hearts are happiest,
For those that wander they know not where
Are full of trouble and full of care;
　　To stay at home is best.

Weary and homesick and distressed,
They wander east, they wander west,
And are baffled and beaten and blown about
By the winds of the wilderness of doubt;
　　To stay at home is best.

Then stay at home, my heart, and rest;
The bird is safest in its nest;
Over all that flutter their wings and fly
A hawk is hovering in the sky;
　　To stay at home is best.

HENRY WADSWORTH LONGFELLOW

A Superscription

Look in my face; my name is Might-have-been;
I am also called No-more, Too-late, Farewell;
Unto thine ear I hold the dead-sea-shell
Cast up thy Life's foam-fretted feet between;
Unto thine eyes the glass where that is seen
Which had Life's form and Love's, but by my spell
Is now a shaken shadow intolerable,
Of ultimate things unuttered the frail screen.
Mark me, how still I am! But should there dart
One moment through thy soul the soft surprise
Of that winged Peace which lulls the breath of sighs,—
Then shalt thou see me smile, and turn apart
Thy visage to mine ambush at thy heart
Sleepless with cold commemorative eyes.

DANTE GABRIEL ROSSETTI

Who Would Have Thought?

Who would have thought my shrivelled heart
Could have recovered greenness? It was gone
　Quite under ground, as flowers depart
To feed their mother-root when they have blown;
　　Where they together
　　All the hard weather,
　Dead to the world, keep house unknown.

Dead are thy wonders, Lord of Power,
Killing and quickening, bringing down to hell
　And up to heaven in an hour;
Making a chiming of a passing bell.
　　We say amiss,
　　This or that is:
　Thy word is all, if we could spell.

And now in age I bud again;
After so many deaths I live and write;
　I once more smell the dew and rain,

And relish versing: O my only Light,
　　It cannot be
　　That I am he
On whom thy tempest fell all night.

GEORGE HERBERT

Fortune

Enid's Song

Turn, Fortune, turn thy wheel and lower the proud;
Turn thy wild wheel through sunshine, storm, and cloud;
Thy wheel and thee we neither love nor hate.

Turn, Fortune, turn thy wheel with smile or frown;
With that wild wheel we go not up or down;
Our hoard is little, but our hearts are great.

Smile and we smile, the lords of many lands;
Frown and we smile, the lords of our own hands;
For man is man and master of his fate.

Turn, turn they wheel above the staring crowd;
Thy wheel and thou are shadows in the cloud;
Thy wheel and thee we neither love nor hate.

ALFRED, LORD TENNYSON

Jenny Kiss'd Me

Jenny kiss'd me when we met,
    Jumping from the chair she sat in;
Time, you thief, who love to get
    Sweets into your list, put that in!
Say I'm weary, say I'm sad,
    Say that health and wealth have miss'd me,
Say I'm growing old, but add,
    Jenny kiss'd me.

LEIGH HUNT

A Death Blow Is a Life Blow

A Death blow is a Life blow to Some
Who till they died, did not alive become—
Who had they lived, had died but when
They died, Vitality begun.

EMILY DICKINSON

Our Revels Now Are Ended

From "The Tempest"

> Our revels now are ended. These our actors,
> As I foretold you, were all spirits and
> Are melted into air, into thin air:
> And, like the baseless fabric of this vision,
> The cloud-capp'd towers, the gorgeous palaces,
> The solemn temples, the great globe itself,
> Yea, all which it inherit, shall dissolve
> And, like this insubstantial pageant faded,
> Leave not a rack behind. We are such stuff
> As dreams are made on, and our little life
> Is rounded with a sleep.

WILLIAM SHAKESPEARE

Written in Northampton County Asylum

I am! yet what I am who cares, or knows?
   My friends forsake me like a memory lost.
I am the self-consumer of my woes;
   They rise and vanish, an oblivious host,
Shadows of life, whose very soul is lost.
And yet I am—I live—though I am toss'd

Into the nothingness of scorn and noise,
   Into the living sea of waking dream,
Where there is neither sense of life, nor joys,
   But the huge shipwreck of my own esteem
And all that's dear. Even those I loved the best
Are strange—nay, they are stranger than the rest.

I long for scenes where man has never trod—
   For scenes where woman never smiled or wept—
There to abide with my Creator, God,
   And sleep as I in childhood sweetly slept,
Full of high thoughts, unborn. So let me lie,—
The grass below; above, the vaulted sky.

JOHN CLARE

Prelude to the Voices of the Night

Pleasant it was, when woods were green,
  And winds were soft and low,
To lie amid some sylvan scene,
Where, the long drooping boughs between,
Shadows dark and sunlight sheen
  Alternate come and go;

Or where the denser grove receives
  No sunlight from above,
But the dark foliage interweaves
In one unbroken roof of leaves,
Underneath whose sloping eaves
  The shadows hardly move.

Beneath some patriarchal tree
  I lay upon the ground;
His hoary arms uplifted he,
And all the broad leaves over me
Clapped their little hands in glee,
  With one continuous sound;—

A slumberous sound, a sound that brings
  The feelings of a dream,
As of innumerable wings,
As, when a bell no longer swings,
Faint the hollow murmur rings
  O'er meadow, lake, and stream.

And dreams of that which cannot die,
  Bright visions, came to me,
As lapped in thought I used to lie,
And gaze into the summer sky,
Where the sailing clouds went by,
  Like ships upon the sea;

Dreams that the soul of youth engage
  Ere Fancy has been quelled;
Old legends of the monkish page,
Traditions of the saint and sage,
Tales that have the rime of age
  And chronicles of eld.

And, loving still these quaint old themes,
  Even in the city's throng
I feel the freshness of the streams
That, crossed by shades and sunny gleams,
Water the green land of dreams,
  The holy land of song.

HENRY WADSWORTH LONGFELLOW

The Sculptor

I took a piece of plastic clay
And idly fashioned it one day,
And as my fingers pressed it, still
It bent and yielded to my will.

I came again, when days were passed,
The bit of clay was hard at last,
The form I gave it, still it bore,
But I could change that form no more.

Then I took a piece of *living* clay
And gently formed it, day by day
And molded with my power and art,
A young child's soft and yielding heart.
I came again when years were gone,
It was a *man* I looked upon.
He still that early impress bore,
And I could change it, nevermore.

AUTHOR UNKNOWN